John Adair is currently visiting Professor in Leadership Studies at the University of Exeter and an international consultant to a wide variety of organizations in business, government, the voluntary sector, education and health. He has been named as one of the forty people worldwide who have contributed most to the development of management thought and practice.

Educated at St Paul's School, John Adair has enjoyed a varied and colourful career. He served in the Arab Legion, worked as a deckhand on an Arctic trawler and had a spell as an orderly in a hospital operating theatre. After Cambridge he became senior lecturer in Military History and Leadership Training Adviser at the Royal Military Academy, Sandhurst before becoming Director of Studies at St George's House in Windsor Castle and then Assistant Director of the Industrial Society. Later he became the world's first professor in Leadership Studies at the University of Surrey. He now writes extensively on leadership, management and history, as well as working as an international consultant.

John Adair is married with three children. He lives near Guildford in Surrey.

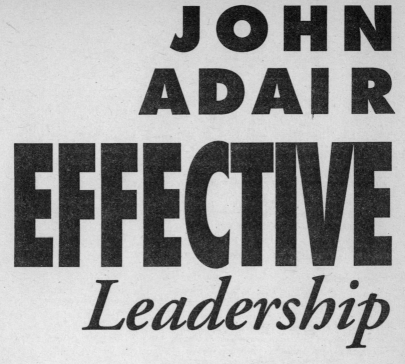

JOHN ADAIR

EFFECTIVE

Leadership

How to develop leadership skills

PAN BOOKS

First published 1983 by Gower Publishing Co Ltd

This edition published 1988 by Pan Books
an imprint of Macmillan General Books
25 Eccleston Place, London SW1W 9NF
and Basingstoke

Associated companies throughout the world

ISBN 0 330 30230 2

Copyright © John Adair 1983, 1988

The right of John Adair to be identified as the
author of this work has been asserted by him in accordance
with the Copyright, Designs and Patents Act 1988.

19 18 17 16 15 14 13

A CIP catalogue record for this book is available from
the British Library

Printed and bound in Great Britain

To my father
Robin Adair

Contents

page

INTRODUCTION   1

PART ONE: UNDERSTANDING LEADERSHIP

1 What you have to be or become   7
2 What you have to know or learn   15
3 What you have to do   26
4 Pulling the threads together   49
5 Some practical applications   62

PART TWO: DEVELOPING YOUR LEADERSHIP ABILITIES

6 Defining the task   77
7 Planning   83
8 Briefing   93
9 Controlling   105
10 Evaluating   114
11 Motivating   129
12 Organising   142
13 Setting an example   159

PART THREE: GROWING AS A LEADER

14 Does your organisation develop leaders?   169
15 Your leadership self-development programme   188

APPENDICES

1 Answers to exercises   201
2 Analysis of a leadership situation   206

REFERENCES   213
LEADERSHIP DEVELOPMENT RESOURCES   217
INDEX   219

Introduction

Ideas about leadership have changed considerably in recent times. People today are better educated and more articulate. They can no longer be commanded in the same way as before. In industry trade unions are certainly more vigilant and often more militant. There needs to be much more involvement and participation at work – everyone recognises that fact. But to achieve these ends industry has to see its managers more as leaders. Indeed, every kind of working enterprise has acknowledged that it needs more and better leadership at all levels. How can it be developed?

THE BOOK'S AIM

The aim of this book is to help you to improve your own abilities as a leader. I am assuming that you have a direct personal interest in leadership. You may be in a position which you suspect – or have been told – requires leadership. You may already be an experienced leader, or you may be on the threshold of a career in management which will expect you to become a leader. In each case

LEADERSHIP MATTERS TO YOU.

How can you improve your leadership ability?

1 *You need to stimulate your own AWARENESS of leadership in all its aspects*. That means being aware when it is required in a given situation and aware when it is lacking. It also entails an awareness of the changing values of society (and industry which reflects those values) which will deepen your awareness of the importance of good leadership if free men and women are to co-operate effectively.

2 *You need to establish your UNDERSTANDING of the principles, requirements or functions of leadership.* The poor leadership of many managers can be attributed, in part, to ignorance. No one ever told them the functions of leadership. So they miss out some vital factor. A good leader understands the whole spectrum of leadership behaviour, and knows when a given function is required. .

3 *You need to develop your SKILLS in providing the necessary functions.* This book will give you guidance not only on *when* to do a particular action, and *why* it should be done, but also *how* it should be done. It is concerned with techniques in a wide sense, namely the *methods* you must practise in order to achieve your desired aim of becoming a better leader. But this book will not teach you much about techniques in the narrower sense – the formal or mechanical tricks which are often taught at the expense of the art of leadership as a whole. Concentrate on the basics – and leave the tricks-of-the-trade to the charlatans!

HOW TO USE THIS BOOK

In order to get the most from this book it is best to read it once to get a general understanding. Then go back and work through the checklist questions and exercises. If you can persuade a friend or colleague to monitor your answers, so much the better.

Do not assume you have to start from the beginning and read through to the end. The book is organised to move from the *general* to the more *particular*, from the whole to the specific parts. Some people prefer to learn by starting off with the particular (e.g. drills, skills or techniques) and moving to general. If you belong to this group it may be better for you to start with Part Two and work hard on that, then read Part One. The more general ideas, which can be found in Part Three, are designed to stimulate further thought. You may also prefer to complete the *checklists* at the end of most chapters *before* reading the chapter rather than afterwards. Decide your strategy for using the book now, according to your depth of interest and preferred method of learning.

HOW WE LEARN

It is irrelevant which approach you adopt or how carefully you read the book; you will learn nothing about leadership unless you make a conscious effort to relate the points to your real life experience. It is essential to bear in mind that people learn by the interaction of

PRINCIPLES		**EXPERIENCE**
or	and	or
THEORY		**PRACTICE**

It is when sparks jump between these two poles – the general and the actual – that learning occurs. So you need both. The various case-studies and examples in this book are designed to be *stepping-stones*:

PRINCIPLES	➤	**THIRD-PERSON EXAMPLES**	➤	**YOUR EXPERIENCE**

Equally the process must work in reverse. Your practical knowledge, gleaned from both observation of actual leaders and your own practical experience, must be brought to bear in a *constructively critical* way on the ideas presented in this book.

Therefore read the book reflectively. Put it down occasionally and work on some *incidents* in your own career which are illuminated by the book, for personal reflections will illustrate better than any second-hand case-study leadership lessons.

The value of having some theory or principles, guidelines or checklists of leadership, is that they will cut down the time you take to learn from experience. As Henry Ford said, 'By the time a man is ready to graduate from the University of Experience he is too old to work!' George Bernard Shaw added that the fees you have to pay in that hard school are exceptionally high! Nothing can prevent you from making your own mistakes, for book learning is not the same as practical wisdom. But trial-and-error is certainly an expensive and over-long way of learning about leadership: it is cheaper and saves time if you learn from other people's mistakes. The beginner in leadership should look upon this book as a *sketch-map* of an undiscovered country. The real terrain will not always look like the rough map in his hand. In time he will be able to draw a better map, but at least it is a guide.

Nothing can rival what we learn by experience. This book may not teach the veteran leader anything new, but it may help him to place in better order what he knows already, so that he can make better use of it. The three-circles diagram (on p. 33) is especially valuable here. It serves as the core of my own understanding of leadership.

USING THE BOXES

This book is primarily a practical guide, but I hope that it will also be enjoyed. To supplement the main body of the text I have introduced in the boxes what amounts to a small anthology on leadership. My main objective in doing so is to stimulate further thought by giving some tangible examples of what proven and often famous leaders have done or said. Some have appeared in my earlier book *Training for Leadership* (1968), but I have called them into service again because they are classic illustrations. I have boxed them so that if you like you can omit them altogether without missing the main points, but the effort on your part to relate the examples in the boxes to the ideas in the text should prove rewarding. This may be a further exercise you could set yourself at the end of your preliminary reading.

You will notice that I have chosen to quote mainly from actual leaders rather than from academics, because I find them far more useful. But the fact that some of these pieces are by military men calls for comment. Am I advocating a military style of leadership in industry? Of course not. But the raw materials of leadership are the same in any profession. I am assuming that you have sufficient creative intelligence to search for lessons about leadership in areas other than your own work sphere. There is a *principle* or general method in these examples from history or another field which is relevant to you. You have to identify that principle with my help and *transfer* or translate it into the language of industry. I hope that the examples I give will prompt you to start your own anthology of leadership, as a personal supplement to these pages.

In summary, by the time you have finished the book I hope to have aroused or deepened your interest in leadership, to have persuaded you that there is an inner core or structure to it, and to have prompted you to see ways in which you can develop your own ability to the full.

Part One
UNDERSTANDING
LEADERSHIP

Understanding for most people is the key that unlocks the door of action. You need to know about the findings of research in this field and to accept or formulate some general or integrated concept of leadership. This knowledge can serve as a guide or sketch-map as you explore further the question of leadership later in the book.

By the time you have finished reading the sections and working on the various checklists, exercises and case-studies in Part One, you should:

1 know the three main approaches to leadership and be able to see how they fit together into the general theory of FUNCTIONAL LEADERSHIP based upon the three-circles diagram (see p. 33)
2 have become more AWARE of how the three areas of TASK, GROUP and INDIVIDUAL interact upon each other for good or ill
3 appreciate the PRACTICAL APPLICATIONS of the general theory to the selection and training of leaders in the public services and industry.

1 What You Have To Be or Become

It is a fact that some men possess an inbred superiority which gives them a dominating influence over their contemporaries, and marks them out unmistakably for leadership. This phenomenon is as certain as it is mysterious. It is apparent in every association of human beings in every variety of circumstances and on every plane of culture. In a school among boys, in a college among the students, in a factory, shipyard, or a mine among the workmen, as certainly as in the Church and in the Nation, there are those who, with an assured and unquestioned title, take the leading place, and shape the general conduct.

So declared an eminent lecturer on leadership before the University of St. Andrews in 1934. Since time immemorial people have sought to understand this natural phenomenon of leadership. What is it that gives a person this influence over his fellows?

As this lecturer believed, most people thought that leadership was an 'inbred superiority' – in other words, you are either born with it or not. The born leader will emerge naturally as the leader because his qualities of mind, spirit and character give him that 'assured and unquestioned title'. Since 1934 quite a lot of leaders, observers of leaders, and trainers of leaders have been prepared to list the qualities which they believe constitute born leadership. The difficulty is that the lists vary considerably, even allowing for the fact that the compilers are often using rough synonyms for the same trait. Also they become rather long. In fact there is a bewildering number of trait names from which the student of leadership could make up his portfolio. Two researchers have compiled a list of some 17,000 words which can be used for describing personality.[1]

A study by Professor C. Bird of the University of Minnesota in 1940 looked at 20 experimental investigations into leadership and found that only 5 per cent of the traits appear in three or more of the lists.[2]

A questionnaire-survey of 75 top executives, carried out by the American business journal, *Fortune*, listed fifteen executive qualities: judgement, initiative, integrity, foresight, energy, drive, human relations skill, decisiveness, dependability, emotional stability, fairness, ambition, dedication, objectivity and cooperation. Nearly a third of the 75 said that they thought all these qualities were indispensable. The replies showed that these personal qualities have no generally-accepted meaning. For instance, the definitions of dependability included 147 different concepts. Some executives even gave as many as eight or nine.

Apart from this apparent confusion, there is a second drawback to the qualities or traits approach. It does not form a good basis for leadership development. 'Smith is not a born leader yet', wrote one manager about his subordinate. What can the manager do about it? What can Smith do? The assumption that leaders are born and not made favours an emphasis upon *selection* rather than *training* for leadership. It tends to favour early identification of those with the silver spoon of innate leadership in their mouths and it breeds the attitude 'You cannot teach leadership', but that assumption has now been challenged and proven to be false.

It would be wrong, however, to dismiss the qualities approach altogether. It has been the custom to do so among academic social scientists studying leadership for two broad reasons. First, they could not invent the necessary instruments for scientifically identifying such intangibles as qualities of character, nor is it likely that they will do so. That is why the historian will always have as much to teach us about leadership as the behavioural scientist. Secondly, value judgements or hidden assumptions crept into the story. Social scientists tend to be strongly egalitarian. They dislike any idea that a person might have an 'inbred superiority' over another. Therefore they are apt to discountenance the whole notion of leadership exercised by one person.

Choosing a new leader

Volunteers to man the new Penlee lifeboat, which will replace the one lost with all its crew a week ago, will start rigorous training this week. Twenty-five volunteers have come forward from the Cornish village of Mousehole where the dead crew members were based and will train under Leslie Visponds, of the RNLI.

In all, 16 people are believed to have died; eight crew members and the eight people aboard the coaster Union Star which the lifeboat was trying to rescue when it smashed into it. A government inquiry has begun into the disaster.

The man most likely to lead the new crew is Mike Sutherland, an experienced local seaman and Trinity House pilot; but the ultimate selection of the coxswain will depend on the training.

Visponds said yesterday: "As the training proceeds, one man or maybe two will show that they have the right qualities and the right temperament to act as leader under the most difficult conditions, and the best crew members will also emerge.

It is up to them to indicate who they would like to lead them, and I am hopeful that I shall be able to ratify their selection and choice."

Press Report, December 1981

But we do know some things about the characteristics of leaders. Leaders tend to possess and exemplify the qualities expected or required in their working groups. Physical courage (which appears on most of the lists of military leadership) will not actually make you a leader in battle, but *you cannot be one without it.* If you aspire to be a sales manager you should possess in large measure the qualities of a good salesman. The head of an engineering department ought to exemplify the characteristics of an engineer, otherwise he will not gain and hold respect. Thus, a leader should mirror the group's characteristics.

Do you have to be tall to be a leader? Research into these more general characteristics bears out what history tells us. De Gaulle was tall; Napoleon was short. It really does not matter. Some general factors, such as intelligence and aptitude, do emerge from the research.

After a comprehensive survey of 124 books and articles which reported attempts to study the traits and characteristics of leaders, R. M. Stogdill offered two conclusions based on positive evidence from 15 or more of the studies surveyed:

The average person who occupies a position of leadership exceeds the average member of his group in the following respects: (a) intelligence, (b) scholarship, (c) dependability in exercising responsibilities, (d) activity and social participation, and (e) socio-economic status.

The qualities, characteristics, and skills required in a leader are determined to a large extent by the demands of the situation in which he is to function as a leader.

Moreover, despite considerable evidence to the contrary, 'the general trend of results suggests a low positive correlation between leadership and such variables as chronological age, height, weight, physique, energy, appearance, dominance, and mood control. The evidence is about evenly divided concerning the relation to leadership of such traits as introversion-extroversion, self-sufficiency, and emotional control'. C. A. Gibb summed up the message of this and other studies: 'A leader is not a person characterised by any particular and consistent set of personality traits'.[3]

Yet everyone agrees that a leader needs to have *personality* in the common sense of that word. A leader may not be what P. G. Wodehouse called a 'matey' person. But have you ever met a true leader who totally lacked enthusiasm or warmth? Most leaders also have *character*. Someone once defined character as what you do with your personality and temperament, that inherited bundle of strengths and weaknesses. A better

---

Character in Leadership

'Character stands for self-discipline, loyalty, readiness to accept responsibility, and willingness to admit mistakes. It stands for selflessness, modesty, humility, willingness to sacrifice when necessary, and, in my opinion, for faith in God. Let me illustrate.

During a critical phase of the Battle of the Bulge, when I commanded the 18th Airborne Corps, another corps commander just entering the fight next to me remarked: "I'm glad to have you on my flank. It's character that counts." I had long known him, and I knew what he meant. I replied: "That goes for me too". There was no amplification. None was necessary. Each knew the other would stick however great the pressure; would extend help before it was asked, if he could; and would tell the truth, seek no self-glory, and everlastingly keep his word. Such trust breeds confidence and success'.

General Mathew B. Ridgway, later Supreme Commander of the United Nations Forces in Korea

way of looking at it is to say that character is that part of personality which seems morally valuable to us. It is that sum of moral qualities by which a person is judged, apart from such factors as intelligence, competence or special talents.

Whether a person tends to be introvert or extrovert is morally neither here nor there, but we do admire steadfastness in adversity or moral courage and compassion. What is the secret of this moral strength? Many writers on leadership have stressed the importance of *integrity*, which Viscount Slim defined as 'the quality which makes people trust you'.

Not long ago I took part in a meeting to secure better participation between management and work people in a large engineering company. During the coffee break outside the conference room a senior trades union leader took me on one side and said, 'Do you know why these managers want more participation? It is so that they can get us to work harder without giving us more money'. At lunch time I sat next to a top manager. 'Do you want to know why the unions really want more participation?' he asked me, leaning over and speaking in a whisper. 'It is so that they can get more information out of us to use for their wage claims!' Here was an instance of total lack of trust on both sides.

Where there is this lack of trust in working relationships it is often a symptom of a failure in personal or corporate integrity. America forced President Nixon from office because he was judged not to be a man of integrity. 'I have often found,' said Harold Macmillan, 'that a man who trusts nobody is apt to be the kind of man that nobody trusts'.

During a consultancy assignment the manager of one paint factory once told me about his boss whom he said he did not trust. 'Nor does anyone else', he added. 'Why not?' I asked. 'Well, he is a slick operator out to get to the very top. He says one thing to your face and another behind your back. He doesn't actually lie, but he deals in half-truths. He once told me he had read a book about Machiavelli, and by God it shows'. It became clear in our conversation that his boss did not adhere to any moral principles – he was entirely dedicated to his self-advancement. It so happened that I met the boss at a seminar shortly afterwards. He dismissed leadership with an airy wave as 'kidology'. He showed a cynical attitude towards both people and the truth. 'Why should I tell the truth to my people on the way up', he asked me, 'when I do not intend to be coming down again?'

The primary meaning of integrity is wholeness, but it also has a moral sense. It suggests the type of person who adheres to some code of moral, artistic or other values. Prominent among those values is the concept of truth. That is why most people virtually equate integrity with honesty or sincerity. Although it is impossible to prove it, I believe that holding firmly to sovereign values *outside yourself* grows a wholeness of personality and moral strength of character. The person of integrity will always be tested. The first real test comes when the demands of the truth or good appears to conflict with your self-interest or prospects. Which do you choose? By going through such ordeals you are forging your personal integrity – only as iron is plunged repeatedly into fire and then hammered on the anvil does it become steel.

On integrity

Harris: What single quality makes an industrial leader?

Woodroofe: No single quality, but an indispensable one is integrity. No doubt about it. Assuming certain qualities like efficiency, imagination, shrewdness, doggedness and so on, the all-essential one is integrity.

Harris: What do you mean by integrity in this context?

Woodroofe: Most decisions in business are based on uncertainties because you don't have all the information you would theoretically like to have, but having what you have, you must use your judgement and decide. But, and this is what I mean by the overriding importance of integrity, the decision must be made within the framework of the responsibilities the businessman carries. He has responsibilities to the shareholders, the employees, the consumer, even the government of the day. He has to balance these responsibilities thoroughly, justly and without bias. You could, for instance, make a decision which was to the benefit of your shareholders but to the detriment of the community as a whole. *Not* doing that, and knowing why you are not going to do it, and what not doing it is going to cost you, is what I mean by integrity.

    Kenneth Harris of The Observer *in an interview with Sir Ernest Woodroofe, the newly appointed Chairman of Unilver, in 1970*

EXERCISE 1
HAVE YOU GOT WHAT IT TAKES FOR A TOP JOB IN LEADERSHIP?

Place the following attributes in order of 'most valuable at the top level of management' by placing a number 1 to 25 beside them. This exercise can be done by you individually, or with others in a group.

Ambition	Curiosity	Singlemindedness
Willingness to work hard	Understanding of others	Willingness to take risks
Enterprise	Skill with numbers	Leadership
Astuteness	Capacity for abstract thought	Ability to take decisions
Ability to 'stick to it'	Integrity	Analytical ability
Capacity for lucid writing	Ability to administer efficiently	Ability to meet unpleasant situations
Imagination	Enthusiasm	Open-mindedness
Ability to spot opportunities	Capacity to speak lucidly	Ability to adapt quickly to change
Willingness to work long hours		

Now turn to p. 201 and compare your answer with the ratings given to these attributes by a cross-section of successful chief executives.

SUMMARY

The traditional or *Qualities Approach* to leadership suggests that the person who emerges as a leader in a group does so because he possesses certain traits. This view has been rejected by academics. They emphasise the lack of agreement among researchers on what constitutes these distinctive leadership qualities. Such a notion of leadership also seems to run counter to their assumptions about democracy.

Some researchers concede that leaders do have to possess the qualities expected or required in their working groups – the coxswain of the lifeboat, for example, clearly needs to exemplify the qualities of a good lifeboatman. But are there more general or universal qualities of leadership? Most people accept that leadership implies *personality*. Enthusiasm and warmth are often deemed to be especially important. There is also an impressive testimony in history that *character*, incorporating moral courage and integrity, matters enormously.

An understanding of leadership in terms of the qualities of personality and character which one person has to a greater degree than his fellows is *still relevant*, but it is far from being the whole story.

CHECKLIST:
DO YOU HAVE SOME BASIC LEADERSHIP QUALITIES?

List the five key characteristics or personal qualities which are expected or required in workers in your field:

	Good	Average	Weak
_____	.	.	.
_____	.	.	.
_____	.	.	.
_____	.	.	.
_____	.	.	.

Now rate yourself in terms of each of them – Good, Average or Weak. Circle the number where you would place yourself on the following continuum:

Very introvert   Very Extrovert

   5   4 3 2 1 2 3 4   5

(Leaders tend to be slightly more extrovert than introvert on this scale, i.e. they are ambiverts – mixtures of both)

	Yes	No
Have you shown yourself to be a responsible person?	☐	☐
Do you like the responsibility as well as the rewards of leadership?	☐	☐
Are you self-sufficient enough to withstand criticism, in-difference or unpopularity from others and to work effectively with others without constant supervision?	☐	☐
Are you an active and socially participative person?	☐	☐
Can you control your emotions and moods – or do they control you?	☐	☐
Have you any evidence to suppose that other people think of you as essentially a warm person?	☐	☐
Can you give instances over the past three months where you have been deliberately dishonest or less than straight with the people that work for you?	☐	☐
Are you noted for your enthusiasm at work?	☐	☐
Has anyone ever used the word 'integrity' in relation to you?	☐	☐

2 What You Have to Know or Learn

The second major approach to understanding leadership focuses upon the *situation*. Taken to extremes this school declares there is no such thing as a born leader: it all depends upon the situation. Some situations will evoke leadership from one person – other situations from another. Therefore it is useless discussing leadership any longer in general terms. This *situational approach* as it is called, holds that it is always the *situation* which determines who emerges as the leader and what 'style of leadership' he has to adopt.

> W. O. Jenkins published his summary of 72 books and articles on military leadership. He concluded that:
>
> 'Leadership is specific to the particular situation under investigation. Who becomes a leader of a particular group engaging in a particular activity and what the characteristics are in the given case are a function of the specific situation . . .'[1]

To illustrate this theory, let us imagine some survivors of a shipwreck landing on a tropical island. The soldier in the party might take command if natives attacked them, the builder organise the work of erecting houses and the farmer might direct the labour of growing food. In other words, leadership would pass from member to member according to the situation. Note that 'situation' in this context means primarily the task of the group. At one time the Royal Air Force veered towards this doctrine by entertaining the idea that if a bomber crashed in a jungle the officer who took command for the survival operation might not be captain of the aircraft but the man most qualified for the job. Change the situation – change the leader.

This 'horses-for-courses' approach has some obvious advantages. It emphasises the importance of *knowledge* relevant to a specific problem situation – 'Authority flows to the man who knows', as one writer put it. There are broadly three kinds of authority at work:

1 the authority of POSITION – job title, badges of rank, appointment
2 the authority of PERSONALITY – the natural qualities of influence
3 the authority of KNOWLEDGE – technical, professional.

Whereas leaders in the past tended to rely upon the first kind of authority – that is, they exercised mastery as the appointed boss – today leaders have to draw much more upon the second and third kinds of authority.

But technical knowledge is not everything. It is especially important in the early stages of a manager's career, when he tends to be a specialist. As his career broadens out, however, he is concerned with more general skills – such as leadership, communication and decision making. He must acquire these general skills for technical knowledge alone will not make him a manager.

Michael, aged 36 years, had a brilliant career as a 'back-room boy' in the accounts department of a British pharmaceutical company. He had passed all the examinations and specialised in tax matters, winning himself a solid reputation. He had been with the same firm for twelve years. On 'situational' grounds he should have been the ideal man to become the leader of his department when the job fell vacant. When that promotion came his way, however, it took him by surprise. He was not prepared for leadership. The company was in recession; morale in the department was low. He soon found himself faced with all sorts of problems, both about the department's effectiveness and about people, where his expertise in tax law was of no help. He floundered for a while and then in desperation left the company to set up business on his own as a tax consultant.

How far are the general skills of leadership transferable from one working situation to another? The skills are certainly transferable, but often the people are not. For one reason, they do not have the sufficient technical or professional knowledge required for another field. Like courage for the soldier, such knowledge and experience does not make you into a leader, but you cannot be one without it. That does not mean that leaders cannot change fields (e.g. industry for politics) as opposed to making major changes within fields (e.g. becoming managing director of an electronic company after running a car assembly plant), but it implies that they will not be successful unless they can quickly learn the essentials or principles of the new industry or occupation.

Within a given field, such as a manufacturing industry, there are other situational determinants besides the type of product. Size – small, medium or large – is one factor in the equation. Some industrial leaders are attracted naturally to situations where a company needs 'turning around' after a story of decline and loss of morale. Others prefer a lively, technologically advanced company going for rapid growth.

EXERCISE 2
THE ELGA MODEL

David Moreau is managing director of the Elga Group. After university he spent his military career as a radar specialist in the RAF. His career has also included export manager, market controller, founder and managing director of Syntex Pharmaceuticals UK and Chairman, Weddel Pharmaceuticals.

Read through the following case study and answer the questions at the end. Then turn to pp. 201–2 to compare your responses with my own.

'Courage is the quality that guarantees all others.' This is the cornerstone quotation from Churchill, cited by R V Jones, the remarkable physics professor, who, at the age of 29, became the scientific motive force in the successful British Government during the last war. His book on the subject, *Most Secret War*, is a valuable textbook for managers on how great victories are won by intelligence, hard work and inspiration.

Xenophon put it a different way: 'There is small risk a General will be regarded with contempt by those he leads if, whatever he may have to preach, he shows himself best able to perform'.

The application of such ringing, para-military quotations to humdrum industrial activities is more difficult. In my experience over nearly 30 years, there are only three sorts of companies: those growing rapidly, with the problems of change; those whose sales and profits are drifting up at exactly the annual rate of inflation; and those that are sliding smoothly backwards. A preference for energetic action and the entertainment of novelty mean that, sooner or later, I always end up with the first category.

Elga did not require prodding into life when I came there in 1972. The technology of making ultra-pure water and the apparatus for generating it are both still new enough for almost infinite development to be possible. This is particularly so because on the one hand pollution worldwide is increasing dramatically and simultaneously the demand for very pure water in the electronic, pharmaceutical, hospital, food and drink and laboratory fields is escalating very swiftly.

I have found that the problems of change can best be managed by a combination of simple concepts; these include remembering proverbs such as 'least said, soonest mended', and 'a stitch in time saves nine'. You must remember also that change is anathema to 99 per cent of the human race, whether Conservative or Labour, and works like champagne on a very small number of very secure or unusually adventurous individuals. Furthermore, the true opiate of the people is not religion, as the jejune Karl Marx asserted, but leadership. Even at the departmental level, a leader should clearly know what he is doing, and how he is going to do it, while carrying his workers along with him in a way that makes them largely impervious to hardship and painful effort. To allow leadership to bloom down the structure, it seems to me that the simple ideas that I referred to above must include the following:

1 Making sure that your product is as respectable and useful as you can. Few ordinary people want to be associated for choice with a dangerous, useless or poorly made item. In our case, pure water fulfils the useful requirement admirably; although it is difficult to ensure that the equipment to generate it neither leaks nor rusts.

2 Encourage your staff to learn all the time, even if this makes their ultimate departure for better things almost certain. People hate to stagnate, and acquiring new knowledge and skills has a tonic effect. We have French classes in the house, and there is a constant traffic to the local College of Technology to pick up qualifications. Our best company educational achievement to date was a man who got an MPhil at Southampton University after a sabbatical year at company expense and without getting a first degree.

3 Industrial democracy is not as essential as the unions and Lord Bullock have asserted. The overwhelming majority of the shopfloor are not ambitious, and do not want to become involved in difficult decisions – that is what the top executives are paid for. On the other

hand, they want to be consulted and involved by clear and honest communication in all matters that affect them, such as salaries, pensions, holidays, car policies, working hours and health and safety at work. For this reason, we have a Health, Safety and Welfare Committee weighted towards the shop floor, where any aspect of the company's activities can be discussed, and actions will be taken if appropriate.

4 Since before the time of the Romans it has been known that high morale breeds invincibility. The Commandos, and more recently the SAS, have often demonstrated that belief in their own legend and pride in their exploits ensures that they glory in further successes for the organisation. If the sales department is headed by a gloomy pessimist, a sense of impending defeat can permeate the sales structure. We have made sure that knowledgeable optimists hold the responsible positions, so that their enthusiasm riddles the representatives who travel at home and abroad with a justified belief that they will succeed.

5 Belief in your own ability to triumph is only a part, albeit an important one, of the sustaining of morale. It has many other elements, including a sense of excitement in the company resulting from a mixture of new products, bonuses, foreign travel and perhaps even vehicles one grade above the standard that any particular seniority could expect elsewhere. It is to avoid the dreary sameness that so many American companies hold their sales conferences in Majorca, the Caribbean Islands and Athens. Our conference budget has not as yet grown sufficiently to allow these excitements, but Elga is in any case luckier than most in occupying handsome buildings on a hilltop in the Chilterns from whose 700ft summit you can see Windsor Castle 20 miles away.

Generally speaking, youth has the edge in *imagination and energy* so that a young team has many advantages in doing international business in the harshly competitive modern industrial world. Most of our senior people are in their thirties or forties; but the younger managers are, the more they need real confidence in order to perform effectively in crises. You can only build this essential state of mind by exposing them to the full rigours of their job without 'nannying', but reserving the right to intervene when the situation is plainly getting out of hand; and also by ensuring that they are properly qualified, trained and selected for what they are trying to do; and above all by setting a laid-back, disciplined but entertaining style for the company. As Lord Chalfont said the other day: *'People who are incapable of relaxing should never be placed in positions of responsibility'*.

If this odd assortment of attitudes is applied, what can you hope to get? Elga has grown from a turnover of £400,000 in 1972 to expected total sales of £4,000,000 in the 1980 financial year. Discounting inflation – and part of the trick of not going to the wall nowadays is always to do so – this is a real growth in sales of about four times, whereas net profits have grown somewhat more, and the return on capital averages in excess of 30 per cent. The company has a stability that would be hard to beat – sales have increased in real terms every year since 1971, and the top people in any department rarely change. It has, from small beginnings, become a leader in water technology, and about 60 per cent of its turnover is exported to nearly 80 countries. And, although it only employs 175 people, they have the complete spectrum of large company duties – advertising, PR, writing articles for a wide range of journals, R & D, shipping and export management, after-sales service, computer operation, putting up buildings, public speaking at scientific and educational events, and personnel programmes including assessment and counselling.[2]

1 In what situations in industry does David Moreau feel drawn to
   lead?
2 In your own words, what are his five principles which have to be
   applied for 'leadership to bloom down the structure'?
3 Do you think the same kind of leadership would work if David
   Moreau was made head of a large government ministry employing
   perhaps 30,000 people and dealing with such matters as social
   security?

Even within a given field – or within a particular organisation within it, the situation varies. Some people argue that such changes require a change of leader. A company in growth may need a bustling, entrepreneurial leader; once it has established its product lines and market share that person may get frustrated and should be replaced by a different sort of man.

A chemical company on Teesside set up a new plant to make ammonia. During the commissioning phase, which lasted several years, there were many crises. The plant frequently broke down; there were accidents and all sort of 'bugs' in the system. Eventually the plant was fully 'on stream'. In the new 'steady state' the first manager who had thrived on the technical challenges became inappropriate. He was replaced by a less abrasive person, who devoted far more time to developing good working relationships which is what the situation now required.

The answer, of course, is to develop as much *flexibility* as you can within your limitations. It is always hard to know what those limitations are. It is easy to make assumptions about them which turn out to be unfounded.

Mark never thought of himself as a leader in a crisis. He worked as a school teacher in South London. On holiday he took a party of boys hill-walking in Wales. One evening a boy who disobeyed instructions and wandered off on his own fell down a disused mineshaft. Far from panicking Mark found himself becoming calmer. He took charge of the situation. After the rescue services arrived and had extricated the boy, they congratulated Mark on the leadership he had shown. He was completely exhausted, but he had learnt an important truth about himself. Contrary to his expectations and those of his colleagues he had revealed the ability to respond to and lead in a crisis. By chance a similar but more serious accident took place in Italy that year, when a small boy got stuck down a narrow well-shaft. Complete panic reigned. Even the President of Italy, who hastened to the scene, could not give the necessary leadership. The child died.

Yet most people discover as they grow older that they are more suited by aptitudes, interests and temperament to lead in some fields rather than others. Let me give a personal example. Like all men of my generation I had to do national service for two years. To a greater or lesser extent we were unwilling soldiers. Those of us who were commissioned, as I was, did not choose to be military leaders, but we were found to have potential for leadership and given the necessary training. As a second lieutenant in a battalion of the Scots Guards in Egypt, I have to admit in retrospect that I was more effective – more of a natural leader – as the battalion educational officer than as a platoon commander.

After some months of service in the Arab Legion of Jordan as adjutant of a Bedouin infantry battalion, I was offered a permanent commission in that famous force by Glubb Pasha himself. At twenty years of age it was a flattering offer, and one which appealed both to my love of Jordan as well as to my 'Lawrence of Arabia' complex! But I turned it down, principally because I knew instinctively that I was not a natural soldier. In particular I lacked a necessary gift: speed of reaction or quickness of apprehension. Like Moses, I am 'a man of slow speech and a slow tongue'. By comparing myself to my commanding officer in the Ninth Regiment at Jerusalem, Peter Young, I could soon see that. He had already won three Military Crosses and a Distinguished Service Order as a fearless Commando leader in the Second World War.[3] Then he had risen to command the 1st Commando Brigade at the age of twenty-six. He had the ability to understand quickly what needs to be done. His mind seemed to work by an instant reflex in the moment of crisis. He was a natural soldier. He sums up his philosophy of leadership in one sentence: 'Leadership is done from in front'.

Apart from good intelligence, basic general ability and aptitude or potential skill in a particular field, leaders who work in situations where crises will occur need this kind of swift mental reaction. Usually training can sharpen and educate it. On 10 August 1981, for example, a Concorde aircraft taking off from John F. Kennedy airport burst a tyre. The captain took the decision to abandon the flight in a second. As the aircraft had already reached the speed of 180 miles per hour he would have been committed to take off in one further second. The broken tyre had badly damaged the undercarriage. The passengers presented Captain Brister with a petition thanking him for saving their lives. 'We practise such an emergency stop on the Concorde simulator every six months', he explained afterwards.

But some contingencies cannot be foreseen. War provides plenty of examples of such occasions when quickness of thought is essential for success. In conversation with Las Casas one day Napoleon reflected on the rarity of this ability to react swiftly in sudden emergencies:

'As to moral courage, I have rarely met with the *two-o'-clock-in-the-morning* kind: I mean unprepared courage, that which is necessary on an unexpected occasion; and which, in spite of the most unforeseen events, leaves full freedom of judgement and decision'.

No victim of false modesty, Napoleon did not hesitate to say that he was himself eminently endowed with this 'two-o'clock-in-the-morning' courage, and that he had met few persons equal to himself in this respect.

EXERCISE 3
WELL, WHAT WOULD *YOU* DO?

Imagine that you are a newspaper reporter in East Pakistan covering the 1971 war to establish Bangladesh. You are tired after travelling many miles on dirt tracks through the hills of Assam, in order to report on the rebel forces in that area. Then you find yourself in a crisis, *one that calls for an instant, effective reaction.*

The reporter who was actually there – Donald Seaman of the *Daily Express* – describes it for you:

They put a boy of 18 up against a palm tree and read out the offence for which he was on trial for his life: MISUSE OF PETROL. Then they sentenced him to die by a one-man firing squad. I watched as the boy pleaded for his life. I heard the click of the rifle bolt as the bearded executioner pushed a round into the breech of his Lee Enfield. The boy was weeping now. He put his hands protectively in front of his face and awaited the bullet.

Petrol is precious to the rebel army in whose ranks the boy prisoner was fighting for East Pakistan's independence. So precious that they count it out by the drop. As a driver the boy had 'misused' the ration allotted to his truck by driving a party of women, infants, and old men to safety. To use petrol even in wartime for such a mission might seem humane to you and me. But to this scarecrow army struggling to set up an independent nation it ranks as a capital crime.

The members of the rough and ready court martial showed not the slightest disposition to mercy. But the soldier who had brought me into the war zone suddenly asked: 'What would you do?'

Every brown face turned towards me. I was now like a judge deciding on life or death in a final court of appeal.

I looked at the weeping boy. He was younger than my eldest son . . .

Well, what would *you* do?
After writing down your reply, turn to p. 202 to compare your response with that of Donald Seaman.

A major implication of the situational approach is that you should select the field in which you wish to exercise leadership with care. Usually interests, aptitude and temperament are sufficiently good guides. With my poor aptitude for music I should be wasting my time to aspire to conduct the Boston Symphony Orchestra. Once you have chosen your field, however, you should aim to develop maximum *flexibility* within it, so that you are the master at reading the changes in situations and responding with the appropriate leadership style. At the same time as you grow in leadership your technical knowledge and experience in that working field should be widening and deepening as well.

Know your field of activity

Another quality common to leaders is their willingness to work hard, to prepare themselves, to know their field of activity thoroughly. I have often heard it said of some individual: 'Oh, he'll get by on his personality.' Well, he may 'get by' for a time, but if a charming personality is all he has, the day will come when he will find himself looking for a job.

I never knew President Roosevelt as well as I did some of the other world leaders, but in the few conferences I had with him I was impressed, not only by his inspirational qualities, but by his amazing grasp of the whole complex war effort. He could discuss strategy on equal terms with his generals and admirals. His knowledge of the geography of the war theatres was so encyclopedic that the most obscure places in faraway countries were always accurately sited on his mental map. President Roosevelt possessed personality, but as his nation's leader in a global conflict, he also did his homework — thoroughly.

Dwight D. Eisenhower

SUMMARY

'Let each man pass his days in that wherein his skill is greatest', wrote the Roman poet Propertius in the first century B.C. As a leader, you should have the kind of temperament, personal qualities and knowledge required by the working *situation* you have chosen. Technical competence or professional knowledge is a key strand in your authority. Yet expertise in a particular job is not enough; other more general skills are also required. These focus upon leadership, decision making and communication. These can be *transferred* as you move into a different situation in your field or change to a new sphere of work. Within your field you should aim to widen your knowledge of the work and develop the general abilities of leading others. That will increase your *flexibility*.

Even within the broad continuities of a particular industry or business the *situation will change*. Social, technical or economic developments will see to that. Are you ready?

CHECKLIST:
ARE YOU RIGHT FOR THE SITUATION?

	Yes	No
Do you feel that your interests, aptitudes (e.g. mechanical, verbal) and temperament are suited to the field you are in?	☐	☐
Can you identify a field where you would be more likely to emerge as a leader?	☐	☐
How have you developed 'the authority of knowledge'? Have you done all you can at this stage in your career to acquire the necessary professional or specialist training available?	☐	☐
Have you experience in more than one field or more than one industry or more than one function?	☐	☐

Do you take an interest in fields adjacent
to your own and potentially relevant?

sometimes ☐
never ☐
always ☐

How flexible are you within your field? Are you:

Good	You have responded to situational changes with marked flexibility of approach; you read situations well, think about them and respond with the appropriate kind of leadership	☐
Adequate	You have proved yourself in two situations, but you fear some situations; you are happiest only when the situation is normal and predictable	☐
Weak	You are highly adapted to one particular work environment and cannot stand change. You are often called rigid or inflexible.	☐

3 What You Have To Do

A third line of research and thinking about leadership has focused on the group. This *group approach*, as it may be called, has tended to see leadership in terms of functions which meet group needs: what has to be *done*. In fact, if you look closely at matters involving leadership, there are always three elements or variables:

The leader – qualities of personality and character
The situation – partly constant; partly varying
The group – the followers: their needs and values

The third school studied groups in a new way. Instead of comparing books and articles on the subject (as the early traits researchers had done), they collected groups together and studied them in 'group laboratories'. An essential feature of this 'group dynamics' movement, as it was also called, which really got under way in America in the late 1950s, was the 'T-group' (T for Training). The T-group met for a few hours a day for two weeks. The 'trainer' and 'observer' set the group no task except to examine their own lives. They declined to take the role of leaders, even under considerable pressure from the group to do so.[1]

GROUP PERSONALITY AND GROUP NEEDS

These experimental uses of small groups for training and research had a profound effect upon the development of *social psychology* which originally concerned itself with the study of small groups as opposed to individuals. Social psychology has produced a massive number of papers and theories about small groups. One of the earliest theories – a general one about small groups – is the most useful one of all for the practical leader – the theory that groups resemble individuals in that they are always unique. We all have different faces and personalities. In practice the phenomenon of group personality means that what works in one group may not work in its apparent twin group within the same organisation.

James Rivers managed a branch of one of the high-street banks in the North of England for five years. He introduced several new ideas, most noticeably for more social activities for the staff: dances, theatre outings and competitions. They were warmly welcomed, and James was asked several times to talk about the successful effect of these innovations on staff morale. When he was appointed manager of another branch the same size in London he eagerly arranged a similar programme, but it attracted no support. Rivers also noticed that many of his favourite sayings and ideas also fell flat on their faces. He felt somewhat exasperated. 'The whole atmosphere is so different', he groaned to his area manager. 'It's as if I have moved to a foreign country! You wouldn't think it was the same company'.

In order for such a corporate personality to emerge, of course, a group has to be in the formative stage for some time. Then its unique character emerges. It acquires something like

Group Personality

It is more important that the Cabinet discussion should take place, so to speak, at a higher level than the information and opinions provided by the various departmental briefs. A collection of departmental Ministers does not make a Cabinet. A Cabinet consists only of responsible human beings. And it is their thinking and judgement in broad terms that make a Government tick, not arguments about the recommendations of civil servants. It is interesting to note that quite soon a Cabinet begins to develop a group personality. The rôle of the Prime Minister is to cultivate this, if it is efficient and rightminded; to do his best to modify it, if it is not.

While a collection of departmental heads mouthing their top civil servants' briefs is unsatisfactory, a collection of Ministers who are out of touch with administration tends to be unrealistic. And a Minister who has an itch to run everybody else's department as well as, or in preference to his own, is just a nuisance. Some men will be ready to express a view about everything. They should be discouraged. If necessary, I would shut them up. Once is enough.

Clement Attlee

a collective memory. Especially when groups are in their formative stages, leaders can do a great deal to set the tone of this distinctive nature.

The other half of the theory stresses what groups *share in common* as compared to their uniqueness. Different as individuals are in terms of appearance and personality, they share in common their *needs*. At midnight all of us usually begin to feel tired; at breakfast time we shall be hungry, and so on. According to this version of the theory, there are *three* areas of need present in working groups:

1 to achieve the common task
2 to be held together or to maintain themselves as cohesive unities
3 the needs which individuals bring with them into the group.

1 Task

One of the reasons why a group comes together is that there is a task which one person cannot do on his own. But does the group as a whole experience the need to complete the task within the natural time limits for it? Now a man is not very aware of his need for food if he is well fed, and so one would expect a group to be relatively oblivious of any sense of need if its task is being successfully performed. In this case the only sign of a need having been met is the satisfaction or elation which overtake the group in its moments of triumph, a happiness which social man may count among his deepest joys.

Before such a fulfilment, however, many groups pass through a 'black night of despair' when it may appear that the group will be compelled to disperse without achieving what it set out to do. If the members are not committed to the common goal this will be a comparatively painless event; but if they are, the group will exhibit various degrees of anxiety and frustration. Scapegoats for the corporate failure may be chosen and punished; reorganisations might take place and new leaders emerge. Thus, adversity reveals the nature of group life more clearly than prosperity. In it we may see signs or symptoms of the need to get on effectively with whatever the group has come together to do.

2 Team maintenance

This is not so easy to perceive as the task need; as with an iceberg, much of the life of any group lies below the surface. The distinction that the task need concerns things and the second need involves people does not help overmuch. Again, it is best to think of groups which are threatened from without by forces aimed at their disintegration or from within by disruptive people or ideas. We can then see how they give priority to maintaining themselves against these external or internal pressures, sometimes showing great ingenuity in the process. Many of the written or unwritten rules of the group are designed to promote this unity and to maintain cohesiveness at all costs. Those who rock the boat, or infringe group standards and corporate balance, may expect reactions varying from friendly indulgence to downright anger. Instinctively a common feeling exists that 'united we stand, divided we fall', that good relationships, desirable in themselves, are also essential means towards the shared end. This need to create and promote group cohesiveness I have called maintenance need.

3 Individual needs

Thirdly, individuals bring into the group their own needs; not just the physical ones for food and shelter, which are largely catered for by the payment of wages these days, but also their psychological needs; recognition, a sense of doing something worthwhile; status; the deeper needs to give to and receive from other people in a working situation. These personal needs are perhaps more profound than we sometimes realise.

These needs spring from the depths of our common life as human beings. They may attract us to, or repel us from, any given group. Underlying them all is the fact that people need each other, not just to survive but to achieve and develop personality. This growth occurs in a whole range of social activities – friendship, marriage, neighbourhood – but inevitably work groups are extremely important because so many people spend so much of their waking time in them.

GROUP FUNCTIONS

The credit for identifying these needs so clearly must go to the group dynamics movement. The very fact of bringing a

group together *without a real task* developed among partici-
pants a new awareness of the need for a task, let alone accomplishing it. So the group threw up its own tasks, and then
analysed – with guidance from trainer and observer – the
contributions of members to these tasks. Far from being
'one-off' acts, these contributions formed a pattern; they could
be interpreted as expressions of *functions* which the group
needed to achieve its *task*, such as

> *Initiating*: 'May I suggest we start by discussing yesterday's
> lecture?'
> *Information seeking*: 'Could we ask the staff for some more
> reading suggestions?'
> *Information giving*: 'I have seen this kind of exercise before
> and it is always best to divide up the task among sub-groups'
> *Clarifying*: 'Are we supposed to finish all these questions by
> five o'clock tonight or can we hand the answers in tomorrow?'
> *Summarising*: 'If I can just pull the threads together, three
> main points have emerged from our discussion'
> *Consensus testing*: 'Are we all agreed that we should work an
> extra hour tonight?'

It could further be observed that some people are more
skilful, or became so, in performing these functions. For
example, an unskilled person testing for consensus might fail
to look around the group for signs of assent or dissent upon
people's faces. So a few nods, grunts or hands raised could
mislead him into assuming that he had found consensus. A
more skilled person would check with his eyes and voice to
ensure that the whole group had achieved a general agreement
of opinion.

Other actions or sentences made sense as *functions* meeting
the group's need to *maintain* itself in some form of homeostatic
balance, so that it was not blown wide open by conflict or
cowered by failure. These functions focused much more on
developing or keeping good human relationships within the
group. The main headings evolved in the 'group laboratory'
movement included

> *Encouraging*: 'We have plenty of time left and we can still get
> the job done – let's get going'
> *Expressing group feelings*: 'I suspect we all feel that we are not
> making much progress at the moment'
> *Harmonising*: 'John and Mike may seem to be making very

different points, but I believe there is some common agreement there'

Compromising: 'If you will concede that we should finish this topic first, then we could take up your suggestion first thing tomorrow morning.'

Gate-keeping: 'Susan has been trying to get into the conversation for about five minutes. I think we should hear what she has to say. Susan?'

According to the group approach theory, leadership was vested in the function, not the person. Anyone who provided a function which was accepted or effective in the group was leader for the moment. The theorists allowed that some groups would have 'safety net' leaders, appointed or elected individuals who would come up with the necessary functions if ho one else did so.

THE AMERICAN DEVELOPMENT OF GROUP NEEDS

The American social psychologists have concentrated on the broader distinction between *task* and *people*. They have spent a lot of time trying to discover the ideal leadership *style*, the relative emphasis which a leader should place on the two areas. This quest then led them back to the *situation*. They have tried to analyse the factors in the situation which require a certain kind of leadership behaviour – for the behaviourist approach to psychology was widely adopted.

Two American behavioural scientists, R. R. Blake and J. S. Mouton,[2] produced a 'grid' against which managers are able to determine if they are more oriented towards *task* (production) or *people*.

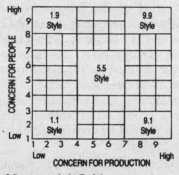

Fig. 3.1 The Managerial Grid

9,1 style   concentrates on the task, ignoring the people 'I get
             the job done in spite of my subordinates'
1,9 style   runs a cosy 'country club', looks after people and
             values friendly relations more than productivity.
             'We have a cheerful crew, but we haven't repaired
             many engines!'
9,1 style   has little concern for people or production 'My
             main aim is to keep my job and stay out of trouble'
5,5 style   is the compromise man who produces as much as
             possible while sticking to the rules. 'Let's not upset
             people but do a reasonable day's work'
9,9 style   obtains high productivity through gaining commit-
             ment. 'How can I harness group energy to achieve
             high productivity?'

In attempting to determine which of the so-called 'leadership styles' would be effective, F. E. Fiedler took into account
such factors as group composition, task structure and 'position
power' – the relative amount of power or authority possessed
by the leader because of his position. His rather complicated
'contingency theory of leadership effectiveness' then led him
to conclude that 'it is obviously easier to change someone's
rank and power, or to modify the job he is supposed to do,
than it is to change his personality or leadership style'[3]. But
his theory and methods, though influential, have not commanded wide assent.[4]

Another more recent off-shoot of the Ohio State University
research into leadership (which confirmed the task/people distinction of how leaders behave) is the work of P. Hersey and
K. H. Blanchard. Their situational leadership theory emphasises the 'maturity' level of the followers in relation 'to a
specific task, function or objective that the leader is attempting to accomplish' as the key factor in determining the relative
emphasis the leader should place on task or relationship
behaviour. Maturity is defined as 'the capacity to set high but
obtainable goals (achievement-motivation), willingness and
ability to take responsibility, and education and/or experience
of an individual or a group'. The authors stress that these
'variables of maturity should be considered only in relation to
a specific task to be performed'.[5]

In fact much of that ground was already adequately covered
some twenty years earlier by R. Tannenbaum and W. H.

Schmidt. In 1958 they published a seminal article in the *Harvard Business Review*[6] entitled 'How to choose a leadership pattern'. They took decision making as their focal point. The degree to which a leader involves the group in decisions, they argued, depends on several key factors in the situation. They include what has been defined above as 'group maturity' – the experience, knowledge and motivation of the group. Several European studies have confirmed that leaders do in fact vary the way they make decisions according to those situational factors.[7] In fact European researchers have followed up the clues provided by Tannenbaum and Schmidt much more than their American counterparts. In doing so, however, they have perpetuated the original confusion between leadership and decision making.

From these remarks you will see that I think the Americans and their European counterparts have gone adrift. Rather than criticise that line of development I want to return to my own. That means going back to the *three* areas of need and an original model setting out their relationships.

THE THREE-CIRCLES MODEL

Teachers on group dynamics courses used a three-circles model to illustrate the three areas of need. It appeared in the duplicated notes which formed the corpus of 'theory' in those pioneer days, but as far as I know it was never printed. So nobody knows who first imagined this brilliant and simple model.

Fig. 3.2 The Three-Circles Model

It is worth reflecting for a moment upon the importance of that distinction between *group* and *individual*, as opposed to allowing them to be blurred together as *people* or 'human relations' or (even worse) the 'socio-emotional area'! European tradition places much value on being an individual. Among Europeans, the British prize individual freedom the highest.[8] Of course individuality and individualism can be taken too far. For we do not become *persons* except in relation to others. But the group laboratory movement in America tended to subordinate the individual to the group. The implicit message was that groups are stronger, wiser and more creative than the individuals in it. 'What the group wants' became the ultimate court of appeal. Perhaps that reflected a sociological problem in America, where traditionally immigrants had to learn to conform – to be 'other directed'. Of course this 'groupiness' was challenged in America during the 1950s and 1960s, for the value of the individual is equally strong in the American cultural tradition as a whole. Although there are cultural differences of emphasis, however, leaders should always be *aware* of both the *group* and each *individual*, and seek to harmonise them in the service of the third factor – the *common task*.

The Individual and the Group

The power of the group is evident too, in its ability to cast individuals into roles to suit the team's purpose. In cricket teams, as in other groups, we find Fun-Lover and Killjoy, Complainer and Pacifier; there is likely to be a Leader of the Opposition, and a Court Jester.

Some find that their only route to a certain sort of acceptance is to play the fool. No doubt a cricket field is not the only locus for their role; a poor self-image may have led them to take this way out since childhood, but the group may push such a man deeper into the jester's part. We had such a player at Middlesex some time ago. At his previous county he had the reputation of being temperamental and difficult to deal with. He became a thorn in his captain's flesh, and a figure of fun to the rest. (On one occasion, when he felt that he rather than the captain should have been bowling, he allowed the ball to pass gently by his boot and hit the boundary board.)

We took him on because of his undoubted talent. Besides, I rather liked him. In our pre-season practice matches, he tended to fall over when he bowled (which prompted stifled laughter), and he presented himself as an appalling fielder (which prompted unstifled laughter, though I knew that we would all be irritated if he fielded like that in competitive matches).

I decided that we should not encourage him to play the fool, but should take him seriously from the start, regarding his current standard of fielding as a point from which all improvements should be acknowledged. A productive rivalry sprang up between him and another bowler in the side. Whenever he slid into hopelessness we reminded him of his strengths. We laughed at him less, and he felt less need to gain attention in this way. Gradually, he spent more time on his feet than on his knees, and his fielding improved remarkably.

This jester's role serves at least two functions; it feeds a (partly malicious) humour in the rest of the team, who can get on with their own jobs seriously and it allows the "actor" a (partly precarious) security. A headmaster tells me that he finds the same cast of characters in each common-room. And families, first of all, saddle their members with limiting roles.

But cricket's range demands these differences, and clearly separates it from a sport such as rowing. On the water, the eight oarsmen have much the same job as each other, and that job does not vary over the whole period of the race. Each oarsman submerges himself in the whole; much of his pleasure derives from feeling part of a beautiful machine. The cox takes over each man's decision-making to become the mind for a single body. But even he has few parameters within which to exercise thought.

A cricket team, by contrast, works as a team *only* by dint of differentiation. The skills, like the shapes and sizes of their owners, are diverse.

So a cricket team needs a range of resources, as does each of its players, and playing together does not mean suppressing flair and uniqueness.

I have said that the creation of a well-functioning team depends on a balance of freedom and control, both within and between individuals. It requires the sacrifice from time to time of personal ambitions in favour of the team's needs. It requires that people take pleasure in each other's success and identify themselves with the team. None of this is likely to happen if respect is lacking. Without respect humour becomes nasty and criticism carping. The side may well split in various ways.

The importance of the group attitude, particularly when orchestrated by a skilful captain, is crucial. It can put players into roles, and cast them into gloom. It can fuel the fighting spirit, or extinguish it. It can foster a harmony of very different skills and personalities, and a competitiveness within a team which may be as helpful as that of the team itself. The path to perfection is not, in my experience, the path of serenity. All things are in flux. The golden bowl conceals a fatal crack. Indeed, like knots in the willow of a bat, flaws can add strength.

Here Mike Brearley, England's successful captain in the England v. Australia cricket matches of 1981, reflects upon the relations of the individual to the group, and the leader's responsibility for building a team spirit which will release the potential of each person.

UNDERSTANDING THE INDIVIDUAL

Individual needs are especially important in relation to motivation, which is closely connected with leadership. One of the things that leaders are supposed to do is to motivate people by a combination of rewards and threats – the carrot-and-stick approach. More recent thought and some research suggests that you and I motivate ourselves to a large extent by responding to inner needs. As a leader you must understand these needs in individuals and how they operate, so that you can work with the grain of human nature and not against it.

In this field as in the others, it is useful for you to have a sketchmap. Here A. H. Maslow's concept of a hierarchy of needs is still valuable.[9] He suggested that individual needs are arranged in an order of prepotence – the stronger at the bottom and the weaker (but more distinctively human) at the top. (see Fig. 3.3).

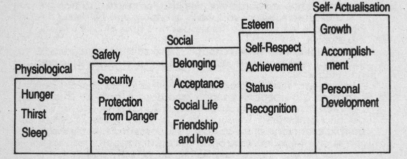

Fig. 3.3 The hierarchy of needs

Physiological

These are man's physical needs for food, shelter, warmth, sexual gratification and other bodily functions.

Safety

These include the need to feel safe from physical danger and the need for physical, mental and emotional security.

Social

This covers the need for belonging and love, the need to feel part of a group or organisation, to belong to or be with someone else. Implicit in it is the need to give and receive love, to share and to be part of a family.

Esteem

These needs fall into two closely-related categories – self-esteem and the esteem of others. The first includes our need to respect ourselves, to feel personal worth, adequacy and competence. The second embraces our need for respect, praise, recognition and status in the eyes of others.

Self-actualisation

The need to achieve as much as possible, to develop one's gifts or potential to the full.

Maslow makes two interesting points about these needs. First, if one of our stronger needs is threatened we jump down the steps to defend it. You do not worry about status, for example, if you are starving. Therefore if you appear to threaten people's security by your proposed changes as a leader you should expect a stoutly defended response.

Secondly, a satisfied need ceases to motivate. When one area of need is met, the person concerned becomes aware of another set of needs within him. These in turn now begin to motivate him. There is obviously much in this theory. When the physiological and security needs in particular have been satisfied they do not move us so strongly. How far this principle extends up the scale is a matter for discussion.

Elsewhere in his work Maslow postulated other hierarchies of need, which he had identified like galaxies in the vast reaches of the unconscious mind: *cognitive needs* (curiosity, the need to find out and to understand) and *aesthetic needs* (the need for beauty, order and elegance). In his later life he also talked much about what could be called *spiritual needs*, the need to escape from oneself and to feel part of some larger transcendent unity above the self. As a secular humanist, Maslow did not give the name God to this welcoming Other in which self is both lost and found, but the influence of the Jewish tradition in which he was reared is clearly evident. Certainly there are great human needs behind the search for God.

Maslow made another significant contribution to understanding individual needs by reiterating the distinction between *instrumental* and *expressive* behaviour. Much of what we do is to meet our needs: it is a means or instrument towards an end. But a person also does or says things to express what he is or has become. A skater or a dancer, for instance, is expressing himself. That can help us to understand why others are doing things. You could also look on leadership as both *instrumental* – a means of meeting task, team and individual needs – and also *expressive* of all that you are and can become in terms of personality, character and skill.

THE INTERACTION OF NEEDS

The three-circles diagram suggests that the task, group and individual needs are always interacting upon each other. The circles overlap but they do not sit on top of each other. In other words, there is always some degree of tension between them. Many of an individual's needs – such as the need to achieve and the social need for human companionship – are met in part by participating in working groups. But he can also run the danger of being exploited in the interests of the task and dominated by the group in ways that trespass upon his personal freedom and integrity.

It is a fundamental theme in this book that each of the circles must always be seen in relation to the other two. As a leader you need to be constantly *aware* of what is happening in your group in terms of the three circles. You can imagine one circle as a balloon getting bigger and another shrinking, or you can visualise the situation as if one circle is completely blacked out. Cut out a disc or use a cup to cover one circle (p. 33) now. At once segments of the other two circles are covered also. Using the disc and doing the following exercise you can begin to develop this *awareness* yourself.

EXERCISE 4

1 Cover the task circle with the disc.

If a group fails in its task this will intensify the disintegrative tendencies present in the *group* and diminish the satisfaction of *individual* needs.

Polymotors Ltd., an engineering company employing 50 people, consistently failed to fill its order books after a change of management. The sales manager blamed the production head, and vice versa. They stopped talking to each other. Morale slumped. Some individuals left in disgust. Eventually the firm failed and all 50 lost their jobs in a time of high unemployment.

Can you think of another example from your experience?

2 Cover the group circle with the disc.
If there is a lack of unity or harmonious relationships in the group this will affect performance on the job and also individual needs.

The Research and Development department in a large electronics firm based in Boston, USA, fell victim to group disunity. Clashes of personality and rival cliques made daily work a nightmare. Through poor internal communication the group failed to meet work deadlines. The creativity of the group dropped to zero. Absenteeism soon increased as individuals found their social needs totally frustrated at work. Eventually the department had to be divided between two others.

Can you add a further example from your experience?

3 Cover the individual circle with the disc.
If an individual feels frustrated and unhappy he will not make his maximum contribution to either the common task or to the life of the group.

Henry worked as a clerk in a city law office. He had been there for more than twenty years and was taken for granted. No one bothered to explain the firm's progress or prospects to him. He felt he should have been promoted some years before, but the job was given to a younger man. Henry also felt bored and frustrated because his suggestions for improving work procedures had been ignored. Gradually he withdrew into his shell. He gave the minimum effort to his work and insisted on leaving the office promptly at 5.00 p.m. He no longer shared his lunch break with his colleagues. 'I am just waiting for retirement', he said to me. But retirement was ten years away!

Can you think of another example?

The circles will also affect each other if there is a *positive* change in any one of them.

1 Achievement in terms of a common aim tends to build a sense of group identity – the 'we-feeling', as some have called it. The moment of victory closes the psychological gaps between people: morale rises naturally.

2 Good internal communications and a developed team spirit based upon past successes make a group much more likely to do well in its task area, and incidentally provide a more satisfactory climate for the individual.

3 An individual whose needs are recognised and who feels that he can make a characteristic and worthwhile contribution both to the task and the group will tend to produce good fruits in both these areas.

Let me give you an example of just one of these three processes, which you should try to match with others drawn from your own experience or observations. *Task* success brings changes in *group* and *individual* circles.

The following case study comes from my own experience. During my National Service I found myself in charge of a platoon of Scots Guardsmen in the Canal Zone of Egypt. We were part of the forces guarding the Suez Canal, which meant for us various guard duties in the vicinity of Port Said. For six months or more the platoon was split up in this way, coming together only for drill or administration. In the summer the whole battalion moved south to guard a vast ammunition dump in the flat desert waste. My platoon was given the job of laying a thick and broad wire barrier around a section of this place. We had to drive out to the place in a lorry with all the supplies, and then start work where our predecessors had left off. The dump was so large that we were almost out of sight from any buildings.

On the first day we laid about 200 yards of wire. It was extremely hot and the soldiers did not look especially happy. Next day I took my shirt off and worked with the men, twisting wire and knocking in stakes. By teatime we had put down 300 yards of entanglements. That evening I worked out several ways of doing the job faster, such as dumping stores in advance of the work, and again next day we laid more wire. By the fourth day a remarkable change had come over the platoon: they were cheerful, keen, full of ideas, reluctant to stop work and eager to set a higher target for the fifth day. So it continued for ten days.

I noticed a big change in Guardsman McCluskey, a real troublemaker back in barracks. Here he emerged as a leader of a sub-group. He was enthusiastically still talking about ways of laying more wire if we could be allowed to obtain certain other types of equipment when the time came to hand over the job to the next platoon. 'You'll never lay 700 yards of wire in a day like *we* have done', announced McCluskey to the newcomers. Nor did they! Although I carried the scars of the barbed wire on my arms for several years, I looked back upon those days under the burning sun as not only happy ones, but also as extremely significant for my understanding of leadership.

Incidentally, I had much the same job to do with Bedouin soldiers when I was in the Arab Legion, this time under more hazardous conditions. The Bedouins responded just as well. As Lawrence of Arabia said, 'the Bedouins are hard to drive but easy to lead'. Aren't we all?

EXERCISE 5

1 Can you give an example from your experience where the *group* circle has been exceptionally good – real team spirit, plenty of synergy, excellent personal relations and good communication – and has enabled it to deal positively with *task* factors that would have defeated a less capable group? What have been the effects of such a group on the *individual* within it – think of a particular case known to you.

Techcom Ltd, a small firm of 150 people in Surrey, had built up excellent working relations and morale was extremely high. Management and employees trusted each other and liked working together; they believed in the future of their industry and wanted to expand. In 1981 they were hit by the worst recession for years and some fierce competition from Korea. The employees volunteered to take a cut in their wages; the management promised there would be no redundancies if they could help it. Everyone redoubled their efforts. Soon business improved again and they were back in profit.

2 Add now an example where an *individual* has effectively influenced the *task* circle and also benefited the *group* as a whole.

Outstanding examples of the influence of the *individual* on the other two circles are often provided by two kinds of members – *leaders* and *creative thinkers*. These may be united in the same person, often called an *entrepreneur*, or they may exist separately. Certainly every group needs its creative thinkers, whether they are managers or not.

'Just a piece of basic thinking'

Plessey had a licence to manufacture an American-designed self-sealing coupling and I suggested we could develop our own. I was told they 'weren't interested'. The frustration this bred in Michael Moore led him to start his own company – High Temperature Engineers of Fareham in the United Kingdom.

Sub-contract work provided the bread and butter to keep the workshop going while Moore perfected his self-sealing coupling. "If you get water in a hydraulic system you have trouble, if you get any air in, you have worse trouble because the controls will go spongy. So when you're testing the hydraulic systems before a flight from a ground power pack, it's very important that you don't inject any air," Moore says.

Even though his work at Plessey had brought him in contact with many aeronautical engineers, it was still hard work selling his concept. Hawker Siddeley was his first customer, using it on the Buccaneer. Later it went into Concorde, the Tornado, the Jaguar and a clutch of helicopters.

His next brainwave was a flexible metallic seal which most people would have thought was a contradiction in terms. "That was a crazy idea I got when they thought they might have problems with the stability of the Harrier jump jet on take-off," he says. The seal, used for flexible air system joints, had to be able to withstand terrifically high temperatures (580 deg C) and pressures (380lb per sq in). Moore admits that nobody thought it could be done. "We were able to machine the metal so precisely that the walls were thin enough to flex. We're still the only people to make it." It is used in most European aircraft.

Moore's reputation for tackling the near impossible brought him a useful line in actuated valves. "Fourteen years ago, when they were building the Jaguar, they came to us to see if we could reduce the size and price of available valves. At that time, they cost £280 each and weighed between 2½lb and 3½lb. We got the price down to £70 and the weight to 1½lb."

The essential breakthrough was the realisation that if the valve could be made to work using less energy, the size of the motor powering it could be reduced. "It was just a piece of basic thinking, really," Moore shrugs. "But nobody else had thought of it. We're the biggest manufacturers of actuated valves in Europe today."

Attempts have been made to copy the valve but Moore argues "We beat them on price because we've got the volume." He would not dream of relying on sophisticated design alone to protect his business. "We must be able to manufacture for pennies and sell for pounds."

Each individual has a piece of social power. That means that he or she can help to build up good relationships and a positive climate at work. On the other hand, by ignorance or design, an individual person can use his influence in a negative way. Hostile or damaging gossip behind people's backs, for example, eats away relationships in the long run as surely as acid dripping onto metal. Gossip as such is an aspect of our interest in people and human nature, and it is mostly harmless. But vicious and unfounded gossip corrodes trust at work. A positive individual may serve the group by challenging the gossipers or the bullies. You do not have to be the leader to do that.

THE POSITION OF THE LEADER

In order to meet the three *areas of need*, as we have seen, certain *functions* have to be performed. Not all of them are required all of the time. Therefore you need:

1 *awareness* of what is going on in groups (the group process or underlying behaviour as well as the tip of the iceberg – the actual content of the discussion).
2 Then you need *understanding* which means in this context knowing that a particular function is required.
3 You should have the *skill* to do it well enough to be effective. That can usually be judged by whether or not the group responds or changes course.

But are these membership or leadership functions? The orthodox teaching of the group laboratory movement, as we have seen, was somewhat ambiguous on this point. On the whole they were happier talking about leadership rather than leaders. Leadership resided in the functions not a person. Therefore, the group could share leadership among themselves. If a member provided a function, e.g. summarising, which the group accepted, then in that moment it became a leadership function. If the group did not accept, then it remained a membership function. So leadership passed from person to person, like a ball in a football match. It is true that some groups might elect leaders, but their role was essentially to be as *safety nets*, picking up the functions which members failed to provide.

As already stated, these assumptions rested in part on value judgements, especially the dislike of any idea of an élite of born leaders exercising power over their fellows. It also reflected the particular situation of the group laboratory: 16 or 18 people, all with equal knowledge or ignorance, plunged into a group with no task but to examine their own lives. Valuable as it was for learning or research ends such groups are rather different from real work groups in industry or any other human enterprise.

To begin with, work groups have a more concrete or objective task to perform. Groups which come together to pursue a self-chosen task, such as trades unions or sports clubs, tend to *elect* their own leaders, who are responsible ultimately to the group. Where tasks are given to the group the leader tends to be *appointed* by higher authority and sent to it as part of the package deal. In this case the leader is accountable first to the appointing authority and only secondly – if at all – to the group. He is accountable for all three circles. That does not mean, of course, that the leader is going to provide all the functions needed in the three areas – there are far too many required for any one person to do that, especially in larger groups. If he exercises the art of leadership properly he will generate a *sense of responsibility* in everyone of them, so that members naturally want to respond to the three sets of need. But he alone is *accountable* at the end of the day. It is the leader who should get the sack if the task is not achieved, or the group disintegrates into warring factions, or the individuals lapse into sullen apathy. That is why leaders usually get paid more than the group members.

Fig. 3.4 What a leader has to do

Understanding your position as the leader in relation to the three circles is vitally important. You should see yourself as half-in and half-out. There should be some social distance between you and the group, but not too much. The reason for maintaining this element of distance is not to enhance

The Lessons of Experience

Douglas McGregor was a famous exponent of the 'human relations' school which drew its main inspiration from the Group Dynamics movement. He acted as teacher and consultant to many organisations, including I.C.I. in Britain. In 1948 he was appointed President of Antioch College in America. He had the honesty to admit that he had made some wrong assumptions about leadership:

'Before coming to Antioch I had observed and worked with top executives as an adviser in a number of organisations. I thought I knew how they felt about their responsibilities and what led them to behave as they did. I even thought that I could create a role for myself that would enable me to avoid some of the difficulties they encountered. I was wrong!

It took the direct experience of becoming a line executive, and meeting personally the problems involved, to teach me what no amount of observation of other people could have taught.

I believed, for example, that a leader could operate successfully as a kind of adviser to his organisation. I thought I could avoid being a 'boss'. Unconsciously, I suspect, I hoped to duck the unpleasant necessity of making difficult decisions, of taking the responsibility for one course of action among many uncertain alternatives, of making mistakes and taking the consequences. I thought that maybe I could operate so that everyone would like me — that 'good human relations' would eliminate all discord and disagreement.

I could not have been more wrong. It took a couple of years, but I finally began to realise that a leader cannot avoid the exercise of authority any more than he can avoid responsibility for what happens to his organisation. In fact, it is a major function of the top executive to take on his own shoulders the responsibility for resolving the uncertainties that are always involved in important decisions. Moreover, since no important decision ever pleases everyone in the organisation, he must also absorb the displeasure, and sometimes severe hostility, of those who would have taken a different course.

A colleague recently summed up what my experience has taught me in these words: 'A good leader must be tough enough to win a fight, but not tough enough to kick a man when he is down'. This notion is not in the least inconsistent with humane, democratic leadership. Good human relations develop out of strength, not weakness.'

W.G. Bennis and E.H. Schein (ed) Essays of Douglas McGregor, MIT Press, 1966

your mystique, it is because you may have to take decisions
or act toughly in the task area which will cause reactions to
be directed at you from the group and the individuals who
face, in consequence, some unwelcome change. You have
weakened yourself if you are on too friendly terms, or rather
you have exposed yourself to pressures – 'we didn't expect
that from *you*' – which you may not be able to handle.

There is an especial problem for leaders who are elected or
appointed from among their workmates and remain with the
same group. To exchange the close friendly relationship of
colleagues for those of a leader and subordinates is not easy.
That has been recognised for many years. When the Roman
Army appointed a man to be a centurion (a cross between a
company commander and a regimental sergeant major) he was
always given a century of 100 men in another legion. The
principle is a sound one and is widely applied in industry
today.

You can begin to see why a degree of self-sufficiency is
important for a leader. Leadership is not about popularity,
though it would be inhuman not to enjoy being liked. Because
leaders tend to have social, even gregarious, natures they can
find the inevitable brickbats that come their way hard to
endure. But what matters in the long run is not how many
rounds of applause a leader receives but how much *respect* he
gains, and that is never achieved by being 'soft' or 'weak' in
the task, team or individual circles. See Fig. 3.5 for some
relationships between leader and group.

The leader's social needs can be met partly by relations
with his team, but it is always lonely at the top. He can never
fully share the burden with those who work for him, or open
his heart about his own doubts, fears and anxieties; that is
best done with other leaders on his own level. If the leader's
superior is doing his job he will help to make such meetings
possible (they are often called management training courses!).
Even more important, the leader's superior will himself be a
resource; a pillar of strength and – at times – a shoulder to
weep upon, should the leader require it.

SUMMARY

The third approach to leadership concentrated on the third
ingredient in any leadership question – the *group*. The most
useful theory about groups for the practical leader is that they

Position of Leader in relation to Group		
Behaviour	Useful	Not useful
Leader emphasises distance	Where group knows him well before he became a leader. When group seems to want over-familiarity. When unpopular decisions are in the offing. When taking charge initially of a new group	Where group already has a strong traditional sense of distance from its leaders. When people can be fully trusted not to become too familiar anyway.
Leader minimises distance	When there is lack of communication and trust between management and employees. Where all are roughly equal in knowledge and experience.	Where the distance is already fairly minimal owing to the predecessor's style. Where it can be misinterpreted as familiarity.
Leader strikes balance between closeness and distance	Most working situations.	Where the group needs corrective treatment after either too remote or too friendly leadership.

Fig. 3.5

are rather like individuals – all unique and yet all having things in common. What they share, according to this theory, is *needs*, just as every individual does. These needs are related to the *task, group* maintenance and the *individual*. The work of A. H. Maslow forms a useful springboard into the deep water of understanding 'what makes people tick'. These three areas (or circles) *overlap* for good or ill. Contrary to assumptions in the group dynamics movement, the roles of leader and members should not be entirely confused. Leaders in real situations, as opposed to artificial 'laboratory' ones, are appointed or elected or they emerge – usually a combination of two of these methods. All group members share responsibility for the three areas but the appointed or elected leader is *accountable* for all three. By performing the *functions of leadership* he guides the group to:

ACHIEVE THE COMMON TASK
WORK AS A TEAM
RESPECT AND DEVELOP ITS INDIVIDUAL MEMBERS

Until you can do this essential work your appointment as a leader will not be ratified in the hearts and minds of the group.

CHECKLIST:
THE THREE CIRCLES

	Yes	No
Have you been able to give specific examples from your own experience on how the three circles or areas of need – task, group and individual – interact upon each other?	☐	☐
Can you identify your natural bias:		
You tend to put the *task* first, and are low on group and individual	☐	☐
For you the *group* seems most important; you value happy relationships more than productivity or individual job satisfaction	☐	☐
Individuals are supremely important to you; you always put the *individual* before the task or the group for that matter. You tend to over-identify with the individual	☐	☐
You can honestly say you maintain a balance, and have feedback from superiors, colleagues, and subordinates to prove it	☐	☐
Do you vary your social distance from the group according to a realistic appreciation of the factors in the situation?	☐	☐
Can you illustrate that from experience?	☐	☐

4 Pulling The Threads Together

The three approaches – qualities, situational and group – in the foregoing chapters can be visualised as paths leading up to the summit of a mountain. If you go up one path you will be led nearer to the other two. In other words, rather than seeing them as *alternative* theories you should look upon them as *complementary* to each other. You may be content to hold all three approaches as distinct entities or 'paths' in your mind, or you may want some closer integration of them, a 'general theory' that will reconcile their differences. Academics in particular have quested for such a theory.

> In 1952 C. A. Gibb concluded an extensive survey of research into the subject by stating that 'any comprehensive theory of leadership must incorporate and integrate all of the major variables which are now known to be involved, namely (a) the personality of the leader, (b) the followers with their attitudes, needs and problems, (c) the group itself . . (d) the situations as determined by physical setting, nature of task etc . . . No really satisfactory theoretical formulation is yet available'.[1]

In some respects I believe that the general approach that I have evolved over the last twenty years does serve to integrate or pull together those four threads. It can serve as a good basis for selecting and training leaders on the one hand, or your self-development as a leader on the other.

In this section I shall outline some of the key ways in which I have developed or extended the original three-circles model. In this revised form it serves as the centre-piece of a cluster of important leadership ideas and examples.

One of the differences in my approach was apparent from the start and has been discussed already – the position of the leader. With practical or real-life situations in mind I placed a much greater emphasis on the leader than others who took over and modified the group dynamics approach for management training.[2] Although some people dispute whether or not an orchestra needs a conductor, I have never doubted it. Organisations and groups need leaders. In rejecting inappropriate or bad leaders these American thinkers were throwing out the baby with the bath water. The issue, it seems to me, is to develop the appointed or elected leader's natural abilities (his potential to *emerge* as a leader) so that he can be effective.

As I hinted, some Americans not directly involved in the group dynamics movement, such as William J. Whyte in his seminal book *The Organizational Man* (1955), came forward to challenge the group assumption. The Korean War, where the Chinese effectively used group dynamics to break down and brainwash Americans, had provided some salutary warnings that there were vital issues of values at stake. Yet as late as 1965, the widely respected Professor A. H. Maslow commented in his observations on a group dynamics laboratory:

'What I smell here is again some of the democratic dogma and piety in which all people are equal and in which the conception of a factually strong person or natural leader or dominant person or superior intellect or superior decisiveness or whatever is bypassed because it makes everybody uncomfortable and because it seems to contradict the democratic philosophy (of course, it does not really contradict it)'.[3]

The emphasis on leadership as something exercised by a leader, as opposed to a shared group process, is far from being fully accepted by all academics. But the pendulum has certainly swung back that way in the last five years.

LEADERSHIP FUNCTIONS

Once a leader has been appointed, been elected or emerged, what does he have to do to lead? The early lists of functions, such as those given in the previous chapter, presupposed the T-group situation. Some of them, such as summarising, are obviously transferable to work meetings but they are extremely limited.

In revising and simplifying the list to the requirements of real situations I developed what has come to be known as the *functional approach to leadership*. Later I became aware that this functional approach stood in a historical tradition of thought about management symbolised by such names as Henri Fayol[4] and Chester Barnard[5]. Indeed one of that school, Lyndall Urwick[6], at a lunch arranged by a mutual friend, presented me with a set of signed editions of all his books. But the tendency of this school was to think of functions in terms of *one circle only*, namely the task. They were one-dimensional. By contrast the functional leadership approach sees the functions as touching upon *all three circles*, either directly or indirectly. Moreover, it adds other functions to supplement the traditional list, especially in the team maintenance area.

With experience and reflection each of these leadership functions can grow in your understanding. They acquire depth as well as width. In Part Two we shall be considering them one by one in relation to your self-development as a leader.

SHARING DECISIONS

For many the word *leadership* implies that one person is the dictator: he makes all the decisions and does all the work of leadership. That is wrong. In groups of more than two or three there are too many functions required for any one person to do it all himself. The good leader evokes or draws forth leadership from the group. He works as a senior partner with other members to achieve the task, build the team and meet individual needs. The ways in which this sharing takes place are so rich and varied that they cannot be prescribed. But a leader who does not capitalise on the natural response of people to the three areas hardly deserves the name.

Most practical leaders will accept that other members can help them to maintain the team or motivate and develop fellow individuals. But what about the task? And, in particular, what about *decision making and problem solving?* For these are key activities in the task area.

It is useful for you as a leader to know the options open to

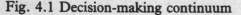

↑ Manager makes decision and announces it	↑ Manager 'sells' decision	↑ Manager presents ideas and invites questions	↑ Manager presents tentative decision subject to change	↑ Manager presents problem, gets suggestions, make decision	↑ Manager defines limits; asks group to make decision	↑ Manager permits subordinates to function within limits defined by superior
1	2	3	4	5	6	7

Fig. 4.1 Decision-making continuum

you in decision making or problem solving. Here, as I have said, I find the continuum introduced by R. Tannenbaum and W. Schmidt a valuable aid. Despite its need for modification, not necessarily along lines proposed by the authors,[7] it has stayed the course. Like the three-circles it has the merit of being a simple diagram. The accompanying article also discusses the *factors* which you should take into account in deciding where to decide. These include the *situation*, especially such variables as the time available and the complexity or specialised nature of the problem itself. Thus, the model helped me to develop a satisfactory understanding of why leadership takes different shapes in organisations which work characteristically in *crisis situations*, those in which by definition time is in very short supply and where there is a life-and-death dimension, such as the emergency or military services, civil airlines and operating theatre teams. Here leaders make the decisions themselves and the group is trained to respond promptly to them without argument. Research at the scenes of road accidents and forest fires confirm that people expect such firm and definite leadership from one man – they need it.

The authors also discuss such variables as the *organisation* (values, tradition) and the *group* (knowledge, experience) which you should also take into account in deciding where to decide. They pointed out the dangers of inflexibility in the leader. The successful leader is 'one who maintains a high batting average in accurately assessing the forces that determine what his most appropriate behaviour at any given time should be and in actually being able to act accordingly. Being both perceptive and flexible, he is less likely to see the problems of leadership as a dilemma'.

Much argument has raged over 'styles' in connection with this kind of model, as we have seen. In the early days these were labelled autocratic, democratic or laissez-faire (or 'do-as-you-please'). More recently, referring to the continuum, they are often called telling, selling, consulting or joining styles. Personally I do not use the continuum to advocate any such style. It is simply useful to show the range of options open to you in making decisions. Research in Europe has confirmed that effective managers take decisions at different points on that scale, for they are taking into account the four or five key variables.

That does not mean to me that they necessarily change their style. Decision making and style should not be confused. Style implies much more than that. Nor is it possible to alter your 'style', which is an expression of yourself from situation to situation – even if you could – without running the risk of insincerity. You do not want to be a manipulator. Speaking for myself, as you will have guessed, I do not find the division into various labelled 'styles' very helpful. It does not form part of functional leadership. Indeed I am very wary of think-

---

On consistency

I recall my late teens when I was a voluntary youth club leader in an East End of London club. Many of the young people came from the toughest and roughest of family backgrounds. On Sunday evenings we encouraged them to hold leaderless discussion groups and we would sit quietly in the background. On the occasion to which I refer one 15 year old decided that the topic should be leadership – he was intending it to be confined to the leadership of clubs but as the discussion broadened and embraced the quality of consistency, he became more assertive about his own beliefs and finally said "I can stand the leader who is a bleeder but to hell with the bleeder who pretends to be a leader". Who could argue with such a fundamental philosophy? This leads to another quality that I look for in a leader: consistency. This is not to be confused with inflexibility; the virtue of being capable of changing one's mind is exceeded by the ability to know when to do it. I refer to the consistency of character behaviour and the maintenance of values. The officer who, in mock battle, orders his troops to attack is not going to get many leadership marks from his men if, when faced with the real thing, his command is 'run'. The words of that fifteen year old are indelibly printed on my mind.

Ann Mansell, Chief Executive of Texales Ltd

ing too much about style. For I believe that style should not be something you arrive at consciously – it should arise naturally or subconsciously as you master the functions or skills of leadership. 'I should like to put on record', wrote Samuel Butler, 'that I never took the smallest pains with my style, have never thought about it, and do not know or want to know whether it is a style at all or whether it is not, as I believe and hope, just common, simple straightforwardness'. But once your personal style has developed, it is as difficult to change as your handwriting. So do at least ensure from the start that it is not confused with any one point on the decision making and problem-solving continuum. As a Frenchman in the eighteenth century said, 'These things are external to the man; style is the man'.

DRAWING UPON THE QUALITIES APPROACH

Such words as consistency and flexibility take us back to the concept of leadership qualities. In functional leadership, however, you can begin to see them in a new light. They can be interpreted as helping (or hindering) the three areas – achieving the task, building or maintaining the team, and developing the individual. First, you should apply the three-circles to all those lists of qualities in order to pick out all the essential ones, those that can be developed. Then some qualities will begin to disclose functions and specific behaviours, while some functions and outward actions will imply or express qualities. Fig. 4.2 shows some examples.

Some qualities are especially important because they apply to all three circles – *enthusiasm* is an excellent example. Some enthusiasts are not leaders, but if you have the gift of enthusiasm you almost always will spark it off in other people. It produces greater commitment to the task, creates team spirit and enthuses the individual.

Other qualities are more latent. They can be called out and express themselves in behaviour in any of the three areas. *Moral courage* and *humility*, to give two examples, are both required in certain situations. But it is important to be as specific as possible in defining when they are needed. Humility may seem an odd word because it implies to many people a cringing self-abasement quite at odds with the self-confidence, even egoism, which marks many leaders. Not so when

Leadership Characteristics	
Quality	Functional Value
Task *Initiative*	A quality which appears in many research lists. It means the aptitude for initiating or beginning action; the ability to get the group moving.
Perseverance	The ability to endure; tenacity. Obviously functional in many situations where the group is inclined to give up or is prey to frustration.
Team *Integrity*	The capacity to integrate; to see the wood for the trees; to bind up parts into a working whole; the attribute that creates a group climate of trust.
Humour	Invaluable for relieving tension in group or individual, or, for that matter, in the leader himself. Closely related to a sense of proportion, a useful asset in anything involving people!
Individual *Tact*	It expresses itself in action by showing sensitive perception of what is fit or considerate in dealing with others.
Compassion	Individuals may develop personal problems both at home and work. The leader can show sympathetic awareness of this distress together with a desire to alleviate it.

Fig. 4.2

you translate it into terms of task, team and individual.

As Aristotle taught long ago, a virtue rests somewhere between two extremes. If you have any quality to excess, or without the moderating influences of balancing qualities, it can become a liability. Certainly too much humility – or rather humility of the counterfeit sort – is fatal to leadership, for it

Humility in Leadership		
Area	Useful	Not useful
Task	When you have clearly made a mistake and you ought to own up to that fact, not blame others	Apologising for oneself or one's performance all the time.
Team	Where the leader is conspicuously lacking in arrogant or assertive behaviour; not abrasive or divisive. Emphasising the group before selfish interest; sharing praise generously.	Showing too much deference or submission to the group.
Individual	Expressing equal value; recognising superior qualities or abilities; giving credit where it is due.	Boot-licking of any kind.

Fig. 4.3

robs you of the proper self-confidence you should have. 'We are all worms', Winston Churchill once told Lady Violet Bonham-Carter, 'but I do believe I am a glow worm'.

Obviously it would take up too much time and space here to work through all the qualities most frequently mentioned, seeing them as aptitudes to acquiring or providing certain functional responses.

EXERCISE 6
MORE LEADERSHIP CHARACTERISTICS

Take some paper and draw a chart like the one on *humility* (Fig. 4.3, above). Now list down one side the following qualities and state briefly when each one is *functional*, i.e. when it is useful and when not useful.

Efficiency	– achieving maximum results with minimum effort
Industry	– energy and willingness to work hard
Audacity	– willingness to take risks that are sometimes large gambles
Honesty	– refusal to lie, steal or deceive in any way
Self-confidence	– confidence in oneself and in one's powers and abilities
Justice	– the quality of being just, impartial or fair
Moral courage	– firmness of mind and will in face of a difficult situation
Consistency	– remaining firm and constant to the same principles

Turn to pp. 202–3 if you wish to compare your findings with my own.

Humility in action

'A sense of humility is a quality I have observed in every leader whom I have deeply admired,' wrote Eisenhower. 'I have seen Winston Churchill with humble tears of gratitude on his cheeks as he thanked people for their help to Britain and the Allied cause'. He continued: 'My own conviction is that every leader should have enough humility to accept, publicly, the responsibility for the mistakes of the subordinates he has himself selected and, like-wise, to give them credit, publicly, for their triumphs. I am aware that some popular theories of leadership hold that the top man must always keep his "image" bright and shining. I believe, however, that in the long run fairness and honesty, and a generous attitude towards subordinates and associates, pay off.'

In a memorial speech on Eisenhower delivered to Congress in 1969, the President of the United States cited as the key to Eisenhower's character an undelivered statement prepared for broadcast over the radio in the event of the D-Day landings ending in disaster. It read as follows:

'Our landings in the Cherbourg-Havre area have failed to gain a satisfactory foothold and I have withdrawn the troops. My decision to attack at this time and place was based upon the best information available. The troops, the airforce and navy, did all that bravery and devotion to duty could do. If any blame or fault attaches to the attempt it is mine alone'.

Dwight D. Eisenhower

At this point you may like to look at the case-study on Gino Watkins (p. 206) in the light of the ideas in this chapter. How did this young explorer achieve the task, build the team and meet individual needs? What qualities helped him to do this work?

THE DIFFERENT LEVELS OF LEADERSHIP

Leadership happens on different levels. Originally work on leadership focused upon the small group. Recently my own work has extended the functional leadership concept to leaders at all levels within the sphere of work, including the chairmen and chief executives of organisations employing more than 100,000 people.

According to the well-known 'Peter Principle', people tend to be promoted to the level of their incompetence. Some people are perfectly good leaders at one level, but they are less able to cope at the next level up. What can help you to determine your own level is your ability to appreciate the subtle changes which take place in the task, the team and the individual as you go higher up the mountain.

The three circles still apply. In the task area the top leader is concerned more with longer-term and broader aims. In the team area he has the double job of building and maintaining his immediate team of senior executives, and promoting a sense of unity among the diverse parts of the organisation. These two jobs are clearly inter-related. Again, the individual for him is both a senior leader – a known person in the senior team – and also each individual in the organisation. The latter will not be known personally or even by name in organisations of more than 500 people, but the top leader still needs to think constantly about that individual – and talk to him whenever possible.

LEADERSHIP AND VALUES

'Is there not a difference', said John Lord (Academy Sergeant Major at Sandhurst) to me once, 'between *good leaders* and *leaders for good*?'[8]

The original three-circles model spoke only about needs. But it is impossible to keep values out of the picture, even if anyone wanted to do so. That is why the behavioural sciences, which properly attempt to be value-free, cannot cover the whole ground. You have values as well as needs and they play a vital part in your decisions. Actually the relationship be-

The Supreme Commander's Task

Because the top leader's team is composed of strong leaders in their own right it can be difficult to weld together. In multi-national enterprises such factors as national pride and self-interest can threaten to wreck unity. Firm leadership by someone with a gift for team maintenance becomes essential. Eisenhower proved to be such a leader in early 1944 when he took command of the allied forces mustering for the invasion of Europe.

After studying the preliminary plan, Eisenhower raised the strength of Overlord's assault force from three divisions to five. He begged Washington for more landing craft, more airplanes. Above all, the new Supreme Commander brooded upon the dismal fate of joint military operations of the past. Historically, the internal hostilities generated by coalitions had produced failures. Eisenhower determined from the outset that the Anglo-American forces scheduled to assault Fortress Europe would become a band of brothers. He had set himself no easy task.

Furtively his generals sniped at each other – and at the Supreme Commander – with depressing regularity. British Field Marshal Sir Alan Brooke, Chief of the Imperial General Staff, complained to his diary that "Ike is incapable of running a land battle. . . ." Field Marshal Sir Bernard Montgomery, often a troublesome subordinate, privately agreed with Brooke that 'Ike was no commander, that he had no strategic vision, was incapable of making a plan or of running operations when started.'

On the American side, one of Lt. Gen. George Patton's staff officers termed Eisenhower 'the best general the British have.' And Patton, himself, speaking off the record, likened Montgomery to 'an angry rabbit.' At one point, confronted by the possibility of serving under Montgomery's command, General Bradley flatly informed Ike that he would resign first. Yet Bradley in his memoirs wrote of the American commanders, 'So scrupulously did we conceal our irritation with Monty that I doubt he was even aware of it.'

At one point, an American colonel in Ike's command had a violent falling out with his British counterpart. The controversy ended with heated words. Ike summoned the American officer.

'I've reviewed your argument and I think you were right,' he said. 'The other man was wrong, and you might be excused for calling him an S.O.B. in the heat of an argument. But you called him a *British* S.O.B! For that I'm sending you home.'

In the end, Eisenhower's dedication to Anglo-American unity prevailed. Field Marshal Brooke even conceded that Ike was 'a most attractive personality.' Montgomery, when the war had ended, thanked Ike, observing that 'you have kept me on the rails in difficult and stormy times; and have taught me much.'

It remained, however, for Churchill to spell out exactly how vital had been the role of the Supreme Commander: 'In him we have had a man who set the unity of the Allied Armies above all nationalistic thoughts. In his headquarters unity and strategy were the only reigning spirits. . . . At no time has the principle of alliance between noble races been carried and maintained at so high a pitch.'[9]

tween values and needs is very close – we need what we value; we value what we need. But they are different. Good and bad, truth and falsehood, right and wrong, profit and loss, are not needs but they do affect conduct.

You may think this is a philosophical point, not a practical one. But the best leaders have something of the philosopher in them. The fact that we are valuing humans as well as needing humans does have implications which are best understood with reference again to the three-circles model. Viewed through the microscope of values we should have to search out answers to the following questions:

Task   Why is this task worthwhile? What is its value
              to society? How is that value measured?
Group   What is the commonly accepted framework of
              values – including ethics – that hold this group
              together?
Individual   Do I share the same values as this group? Is
              the task worthwhile in my eyes?

Some people can do this kind of valuing arithmetic quite easily for themselves. But you as the leader will have to show awareness of the values of the common enterprise and interpret them for people both inside the group and outside it. Task, group and individual have to be related in values as well as in needs. That is why true leadership has an inescapable moral, or even spiritual, dimension. Without it you can become a *good leader* in the technical sense of the word – but you will not necessarily be a *leader for good*.

Leaders for good

If effective work is to be done then there will need to be leadership, otherwise people will thrash around in a fog. Leadership involves, for me, helping the organisation to discover, express and own purposes and values which enable those involved with the organisation to commit themselves to the organisation sufficiently that they will use their intelligence and creativity in its support. That probably means that the central purpose of the organisation will need to be expressed and lived in terms that people can identify with and with underlying values that they can be proud of. Maybe 'to serve the public by producing good value x's and doing so in such a way that all employees are able to use and develop their talents' would be more likely to inspire people than 'to make more profit than last year'? Leadership like this will need to be shown at all levels.[10]

Nicholas Heap

SUMMARY

Functional leadership draws upon a number of traditions but subtly changes their offerings. The well-established lists of management functions, for example, are applied to all three circles. Qualities can be interpreted in functional terms as well. Do they help you to achieve the task? Do they contribute to unity or are they disruptive? But the emphasis on leadership does not carry the assumption that all should be left to one 'leader'. By necessity leadership itself has to be something of a team effort, especially as you move into the higher levels of leadership. Or, to put it another way, your team becomes one which is composed of leaders within the organisation. Your style, which is an expression of you, will emerge naturally after you apply yourself to the simple functions of leadership. For leadership does consist mainly of doing some relatively simple and straightforward things, and doing them extremely well. At whatever level of leadership you are fitted for, by nature, training and experience, you should encourage thought about the task in terms of values as well as needs. Then the common purpose will overlap with the values of the groups and individuals in the organisation – including your own.

5 Some Practical Applications

The earliest practical application of the broad ideas in this book was to the leadership selection field. Before 1942 the British Army relied exclusively on the interview method. A selection committee interviewed the candidate for a commission and tried to identify those with the essential qualities. As you can imagine, this was something of a hit-or-miss affair.

> When Viscount Montgomery was an officer cadet at Sandhurst his Company Commander called him in one day and said, 'Montgomery, I have been watching you very carefully and you will never rise above the rank of major'. 'Well', said the Field Marshal in a talk to a later generation of cadets at Sandhurst, 'he was wrong. It was *he* who never rose above the rank of major!'

In order to cope with the numbers and improve effectiveness (large numbers – up to 50 per cent – selected by this method were being returned to their units from the officer training schools as unfit to be leaders) a team of psychologists and officers devised the three-day War Officer Selection Board. More than forty years later it is still with us (as the Regular Commissions Board) because it was constructed on sound principles.

At the centre of the selection process lay a number of practical exercises. The candidate was put in charge of a small group with a simple task to perform against the clock. The psychologists were aware of the early work in America on 'the dynamics of interpersonal relations'. They had also grasped the significance of the situational approach – not bad for 1942.

In particular they knew that they were looking for leaders who could operate under the stress conditions of battle. While the candidate was leading the group the observers looked at and evaluated (in the words of one of them) the following behaviours:

1 the effective *level of his functioning*: his ability to contribute towards the functional aspect of the common task by planning and organising the available resources such as abilities, materials and time.

2 his *group-cohesiveness* or ability to bind the group in the direction of the common task: to relate its members emotionally to each other and to the task;

3 his *stability* (or *mental stamina*): the ability to stand up to resistance and frustrations without serious impairment of 1 or 2 and the results of their interplay.

In other words, the candidate was tested *in* a group *for* a group. Interviews, intelligence and aptitude testings, the giving of short talks and short role plays supplemented this core of exercises.[1]

Although a number of other armed forces, such as the US Marine Corps, adopted this method, as did the Civil Service and the Church of England in suitably modified forms, surprisingly enough industry on both sides of the Atlantic did not do so. That was partly due to the low premium placed on leadership in management in those days. How many managers in your company would pass a series of equivalent tests? How about you? Here is the chance to test yourself on a Regular Commissions Board practical task.

EXERCISE 7

You have *four* people in your group beside yourself. Jim is about 30 and works in an architect's office as a draughtsman. He was sent on this selection course by his firm to see if he had the making of a leader. He has already failed in his own task. Henry is a rather dominant, bossy man aged 47. He runs his own business. He wears a Scouter's badge in his lapel. Sally is a supervisor in a retail store. Her best friends tell her she is too plump. She talks incessantly. Lastly, Simon is a civil engineer by background, specialising in concrete motorways. He drank too much beer last night and has been sick all morning – besides, it is his turn next!

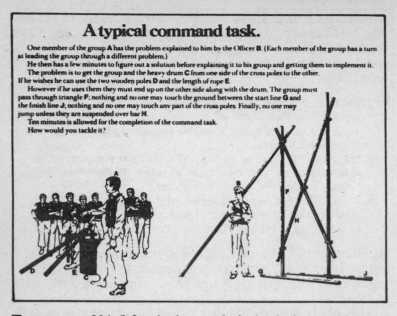

A typical command task.

One member of the group **A** has the problem explained to him by the Officer **B**. (Each member of the group has a turn at leading the group through a different problem.)

He then has a few minutes to figure out a solution before explaining it to his group and getting them to implement it.

The problem is to get the group and the heavy drum **C** from one side of the cross poles to the other.

If he wishes he can use the two wooden poles **D** and the length of rope **E**.

However if he uses them they must end up on the other side along with the drum. The group must pass through triangle **F**; nothing and no one may touch the ground between the start line **G** and the finish line **J**; nothing and no one may touch any part of the cross poles. Finally, no one may jump unless they are suspended over bar **H**.

Ten minutes is allowed for the completion of the command task.

How would you tackle it?

Turn to pp. 204–5 for the best technical solution – and some notes on how the people responded to your leadership!

Obviously if you really did that exercise there would be observers to give you feedback on your functional response to the task, the team and the individual. You have probably been in similar situations at work or in leisure activities – sport, climbing, sailing and so on. Bearing a recent situation in mind you may like to assess yourself as honestly as possible using the current Sandhurst List of Assessment Definitions (see Fig. 5.1). When you have completed it count up your good, adequate and weak scores. If you have more than three adequate or weak ticks you should take very seriously the next section – training for leadership.

TRAINING FOR LEADERSHIP

As a civilian lecturer in military history I worked at the Royal Military Academy, Sandhurst, from 1961 until 1969. There I had the opportunity of evolving, together with a committee of officers, a functional leadership course based upon the three-circles model. We ran the first experimental course in 1962 and Sandhurst as a whole adopted the approach two years later to supplement its traditional teaching on leadership

Attribute	Definition	Scale	
Group influence	The ability which enables an individual to bring about a willing effort on the part of the group towards achieving a desired objective/goal	Good	He was impressive throughout, obtaining a high degree of commitment from the group by an excellent personal example
		Adequate	He managed to convince the group to work to the achievement of the objective with adequate personal example
		Weak	Had little influence on the group almost to the extent that they ignored him
Command	The ability to make up one's mind as quickly as the situation demands and carry through a course of action with firmness and strength of purpose	Good	Came to a decision quickly and effectively and was positive in implementing it
		Adequate	Eventually came to a decision but displayed a certain lack of firmness in implementing it.
		Weak	Unable to make up his mind. Gets confused with conflicting information and hesitant in carrying through his action
Coolness	The extent to which he remains cool and unperturbed under testing or trying conditions	Good	Calm, unruffled and in control of himself. Justifiably self confident
		Adequate	A reasonable and balanced degree of confidence. Comfortable in front of a group

Fig. 5.1

Attribute	Definition	Scale	
		Weak	His under/over confidence seriously impaired his effectiveness and his credibility as a leader
Judgement	Ability to arrange available resources and information in a systematic and commonsense way so as to produce effective results	Good	Shrewd and discerning, he saw his way through all complexities and was effective.
		Adequate	He showed commonsense and judged the task appropriately by producing a satisfactory result
		Weak	His lack of commonsense and poor judgement gave rise to difficulties and he lost credibility as a result
Application/ responsibility	The demonstration of sustained effort combined with the degree of dependability in order to complete a task or achieve an objective	Good	Applied himself thoroughly and energetically to the task showing determination and persistence
		Adequate	Satisfactory industry and general determination to succeed
		Weak	Did not accept responsibility and was overwhelmed by the difficulties that faced him. Showed little or no determination

Fig. 5.1 (continued)

qualities. Thereafter, as Adviser on Leadership Training, I was responsible both for the quality of the two-day course (which was run by company commanders) and also for relating it to practical leadership training in the field. It soon proved that the basic principles in this book could be successfully applied to developing leaders as well as selecting them. Moreover, it lasts. Twenty years later Sandhurst is still using functional leadership to train leaders.

By 1968, when *Training for Leadership* was published, the Sandhurst course had been adopted by the Royal Air Force, the Women's Royal Army Corps and the Fire Service, and two industrial firms had asked me to run it for their managers. The Industrial Society, which had as one of its aims the promotion of good leadership in industry, heard about my work and asked me to establish a Leadership Department. The nature, scope and results of *Action-Centred Leadership* (as

---

Well, can leaders be trained?

Some will say that leaders are born, not made, and that you can't make a leader by teaching, or training. I don't agree with this entirely. While it is true that some men have within themselves the instincts and qualities of leadership in a much greater degree than others, and some men will never have the character to make leaders, I believe that leadership can be developed by training. In the military sphere, I reckon that soldiers will be more likely to follow a leader in whose military knowledge they have confidence, rather than a man with much greater personality but with not the same obvious knowledge of his job. To the junior leader himself the mere fact of responsibility brings courage; the mere fact that by his position as the recognised head of a group of men he is responsible for their lives and comfort, gives him less time to think of his own fears and so brings him a greater degree of resolution than if he were not the leader. I know I found this to be the case myself in 1914, when as a young lieutenant I commanded a platoon and had to lead them in charges against entrenched Germans, or undertake patrol activities in no-man's-land. By the training I had received from my superiors in peacetime, I gained confidence in my ability to deal with any situation likely to confront a young officer of my rank in war; this increased my morale and my powers of leading my platoon, and later my company.

In other words, it is almost true to say that leaders are 'made' — rather than born. Many men who are not natural leaders may have some small spark of the qualities which are needed; this spark must be looked for, and then developed and brought on by training. But except in the armed forces this training is not given. In civilian circles it seems to be considered that leadership descends on men like dew from heaven; it does not. There are principles of leadership just as there are principles of war, and these have to be studied.

Field Marshal Viscount Montgomery

the Industrial Society called it) between 1969 and 1973 I
discussed in a further book under that title.[2] Since then many
hundreds of companies and many thousands of managers
have experienced ACL training. The Royal Navy and the
Australian Army are among the services that have adopted
and evolved it for their own use. Nor is it anchored to any
one culture: the message and language are universal. Ross
Matheson in *People Development in Developing Countries* (1978)
called Action-Centred Leadership an 'entirely dynamic and
realistic' learning approach for management training in developing countries. From my own experience in many companies and countries, I can add that it also works at the
different *levels* of leadership: first-line supervisors, middle-
managers and senior managers.

In a letter to me in 1968, Viscount Montgomery wrote
'Leadership is an immense subject. Nowhere is it more important to teach it than at Sandhurst and in our universities;
in fact to youth, since it falls on dead ground with the older
generation'. Since then, as Professorial Fellow of Leadership
Studies, I have been able to introduce leadership training
courses to engineering students at the University of Surrey.
There is ample evidence that young people destined to work
in industry are eager to explore the nature of good leadership
and have some practical training for it. For there is a wide-
spread sense that 'what industry needs now is not bosses but
leaders'.

The content, methods and character of ACL are reasonably
well known now to those responsible for management or leadership training. Those who want to know more about them
should consult my other books (see page 213). For they were
written primarily for management trainers with those questions in mind. You may or may not have attended – or be
about to attend – a training course. No book can really be a
substitute for such training, because leadership is about
people and they are more easily met and led on courses than
at second-hand in your imagination as a result of reading
books. But you can to some extent look upon this book as
your own personal do-it-yourself Action-Centred Leadership
course. Certainly I have written it with the same features in
mind. These are the characteristics which thousands of managers have said they value in ACL:

Simple	Simple, but not superficial or simplistic; as little jargon as possible
Practical	Concerned with practical, how-to-do-it functions and actions of leadership, not abstract or academic theory for its own sake
Participative	Exercises, case studies and checklists to involve you in the process of learning. That makes it enjoyable as well as useful.

In order to help organisations as well as individuals develop more effective leadership, the Industrial Society has worked out ten guidelines. These are given to each course member on ACL courses. The William Hollings Ltd case study below will give you a tangible example of how one company has put them into practice.

LEADER'S CHECKLIST

1 Set the task of the team; put it across with enthusiasm and remind people of it often.
2 Instruct all leaders in the three circles; make them accountable for teams of 4–15.
3 Plan the work, pace its progress and design jobs to encourage the commitment of individuals and teams.
4 Set individual targets after consulting, discuss progress with each person regularly but at least once a year.
5 Delegate decisions to individuals. Consult those affected.
6 Communicate the importance of each person's job; explain decisions to help people apply them; brief team monthly on Progress, Policy and People.
7 Train and develop people, especially those under 25; gain support for the rules and procedures, set an example and 'have a go' at those who break them.
8 Where unions are recognised, encourage joining, attendance at meetings, standing for office and speaking up for what each person believes is in the interest of the task, team and individual.
9 Care about the wellbeing of people in the team, improve working conditions, deal with grievances and attend functions.
10 Monitor action; learn from successes and mistakes: regularly walk round each person's place of work, observe, listen and praise.

The Industrial Society

If you do look upon this book as your personal Action-Centred Leadership course you should work through the rest of it with pencil and paper at hand ready to write down any *action points* which occur to you. This should be done immediately after the end of *each* chapter – don't wait until the end of the book. The action points should be as specific as possible, focusing on such areas as:

Your performance as a leader
Your own learning and training needs
Points for your working group
Possible changes in the organisation
Longer-term self-development goals

EXERCISE 8

John Gamester, a production executive with William Hollins (Spinners) Ltd., attended an ACL course. After reading the following case study and reflecting upon it, see if you can see any parallels between Wm Hollins and your own organisation or situation. Then list *three action points* for yourself when you get back to work next week.

As a real life example of the benefits of ACL I would quote our experiences at Wm Hollins over the past eighteen months, at the start of which, like many companies, we had major problems in the areas of labour productivity and absenteesim.

Our site at Wm Hollins comprises three spinning mills and a dyehouse where we employ around 700 people who are involved in the manufacture of some of the most sophisticated blend yarns produced by the UK textile industry. To produce these yarns can require up to twenty separate processes carried out in sequence. Buffer stocks have to be kept to a minimum and, therefore, any drop in production at one process, whether the result of a maintenance problem, absenteeism or low productivity, is likely to affect every other machine in the line. Under these circumstances an average absenteeism rate of 18–20 per cent mainly covered by sick notes was a major headache, in addition to which various work measurement studies indicated a lot of potential to improve labour productivity. Our problem was how to create the change in commitment and attitude of employees which would be necessary to improve performance, particularly in these two areas.

In considering the reasons for our problems the ACL card issued by the Society was invaluable in deciding what questions to ask, and what practical steps to take, for example:
● have we made leaders accountable for teams of four to eighteen people?

- have we planned the work, paced its progress and designed jobs to encourage the commitment of teams and individuals?
- have we communicated the importance of each person's job; explained decisions to help people apply them; briefed teams mainly on progress, people and policy?
- have we trained and developed people, gained support for rules and procedures, set an example and encouraged people 'to have a go' at those who break them?
- do we encourage people to join the union, attend branch meetings, stand for office and speak up for what each person believes is in the interests of the task, the team and the individual?
- do we care about the wellbeing of people in the team, improve working conditions, deal with grievances and attend functions?
- do we monitor action and regularly walk the job?

In aiming to answer these questions we have taken a number of practical steps over the past eighteen months to resolve our problems, including the following:

1 *Reorganisation of all employees on the factory floor into work groups of up to eighteen led by a supervisor.*

Prior to this some sections had been controlled by a supervisor and deputy supervisor responsible for between 40 and 50 people. The reorganisation was aimed firstly at answering the question 'who is my boss?' and secondly to give supervisors a chance of really involving their team which we did not believe was possible when supervising 50 people.

2 *Reorganisation of factory management by the appointment of a shift manager on night-shift and one production manager for all three mills.*

Traditionally there had been a mill manager for each mill and shift managers on morning and afternoon shifts but not at night. The reorganisation was designed firstly to reinforce the night shift, which had a particularly high absence rate, and secondly to improve the co-ordination between processes and the consistency of decision making across the three shifts and the three mills.

3 *Introduction of a work study based productivity bonus scheme for hourly paid employees.*

Because of ACL this was made a team rather than an

individual bonus in the hope that it would increase people's awareness that their individual performance or absence directly affected the performance of their team—in short that they were needed. The scheme was deliberately introduced gradually, section by section, so that it could be explained in detail to each team, who were allowed maximum flexibility in choosing how to organise the work of their section.

4 *Introduction of a similar bonus scheme for supervisors.*

This scheme was slightly different to that for machine operators in that the bonus is based partly on the labour productivity of the supervisor's own team and, in order to increase teamwork between the supervisors, partly on the machine efficiency at the mill's bottleneck process.

5 *In-company training of all managers and supervisors in ACL.*

This training was carried out in a series of short courses over the last 18 months, each one of which was designed to be particularly relevant to those actions planned for the following four to six months. The courses were also designed to gain as much feedback as possible.

6 *In-company training of shop stewards in the skills involved in their role as employee representatives including negotiating skills, dealing with grievances, etc.*

This training was run by the Industrial Society since they were acceptable to both ourselves and the trade union.

7 *Negotiation of an absence agreement.*

This laid down rules and procedures to deal with authorised absence, unauthorised absence and sickness, including the setting up of a sickness panel to review cases of persistent short term sickness.

8 *Introduction of a job evaluated wage and salaries structure, incorporating a reduced number of job grades, improved differentials and more realistic shift premiums.*

The previous wage and salary structure had been fraught with anomalies, many of which were the result of statutory government wage policy in previous years. In order to gain maximum support for job evaluation, this was carried out by a committee split equally between management and employee representatives with an independent chairman from ACAS.

9 *Publishing of all performance information by supervisor's name.*

Productivity, machine efficiency, waste, labour turnover and accident rate are all now published by supervisor's name so that progress can be measured and compared with that of other sections, problems identified, and targets set.

10 *Introduction of briefing groups as an improved means of communicating policy, plans and progress.*

These were introduced only after full consultation with all managers and supervisors and also the trade unions after which training was given to each person who was to carry out briefing.

Obviously after eighteen months of hard work the main question is 'has the strategy paid off, is productivity better and has absenteeism been reduced?

The short answer is yes, even though some of the above actions have only recently been implemented the results so far are encouraging, for example:

- productivity is up by more than 25 per cent
- absenteeism has been reduced from 18 per cent to 7 per cent
- labour turnover is down to below 10 per cent
- accidents/1000 man/woman hours have been reduced by 25 per cent to less than half the average for the industry.

Undoubtedly one of the main reasons for achieving these results has been the ACL approach which has helped in a number of key ways.

Firstly ACL training for managers and supervisors has increased everyone's awareness of the need to achieve results through people, in particular the importance of involving their team, leading by example, delegating, enthusiasm in putting across decisions and plans even when they fall into the 'least worst' category, reacting positively to changes, better use of time, and also walking the job regularly.

Secondly ACL has helped us to focus on those actions necessary to give managers and supervisors a chance of achieving the task, building their team and developing individuals. It would have been almost a waste of time to give supervisors ACL training and then expect them to lead a team of 50 people.

Thirdly the emphasis on the team in terms of performance data, the productivity scheme, and the use of briefing groups has helped individuals to see how they fit in and why their job matters. In fact this has been so successful that the absence agreement has hardly had to be used since when any absentee returns to work their workmates quickly let them know how much they've been missed.

Finally ACL has given a common thread to the entire programme, ensuring that each separate action integrates with the whole.

Although all the above comments are relevant, the ACL approach does have drawbacks. These are mainly associated with the fact that ACL raises expectations. Everyone from the factory floor upwards is now far more vociferous in questioning management decisions, they expect to be consulted on matters affecting them and where this isn't possible they expect to have decisions explained to them. Once you start letting people know what's going on and involve them in their work, they expect you to continue, there's no going back – but then who would want to go back to increased absenteeism and reduced productivity?

If your organisation or company does not run leadership courses you can always go on a public one. Even if you have to pay for yourself it is worth it. In Appendix 3 (pages 217–18) are listed some recommended leadership programmes which will appeal to you if you have enjoyed this book. Also in Appendix 3 there is a guide to some books about leadership, some handbooks of management training exercises and some useful feature films on television for self-training purposes.

SUMMARY

The concept of the three circles and the functional approach to leadership have been thoroughly tested. In their early form they were applied successfully to the problem of selecting leaders. My own work has been concerned more with training leaders. This brief review should give you the confidence to apply functional leadership to your own self-development as a leader.

Part Two
DEVELOPING YOUR
LEADERSHIP ABILITIES

The next eight chapters focus on the main practical FUNC-TIONS that you will certainly have to do or manage as a leader. They are deliberately not grouped under task, team and individual, for you should constantly remember that the circles overlap: therefore any function will affect all three. For instance, *planning* may seem to be a task function initially, but there is nothing like a bad plan to break up group unity or frustrate the individual. The functions are the white and black keys on a piano: they will have to be played in different sequences and combined in chords if you want to make music.

By the time you have finished reading and working upon Part Two you should:

1 be able to identify clearly the main FUNCTIONS or PRIN-CIPLES of leadership in the three areas and have a good idea how they manifest themselves in practice
2 know what constitutes SKILL in providing that function in certain kinds of situation
3 be able to establish the ABILITIES that you need to develop in yourself if you are going to be successful in providing those functions over a long and varied career.

6 Defining the Task

Your primary responsibility as a leader is to ensure that your group achieves its common task. Leadership is sometimes defined as 'getting other people to do what *you* want to do because *they* want to do it'. I do not agree. If it is *your* task, why should anyone help you to achieve it? It has to be a common task, one which everyone in the group can share because they see that it has value for the organisation or society and – directly or indirectly – for themselves as well.

Remember that achieving the task is your principal means of developing high morale and meeting individual needs. What you do (or fail to do) in the *task* area is bound to affect the other two circles. So you should bear those two spheres in mind when you commit yourself and the group to task action.

As the leader you cannot perform all the functions yourself. The group is not a flock of sheep – passive, walking lumps of mutton – with yourself as the human shepherd. They can help you and you can help them in pursuit of the common goal in various ways. The group members have energy, enthusiasm, experience, knowledge and ability or skill to contribute to the key task functions.

The actual technologies involved in the task will obviously vary from group to group. But it is possible to pick out some general functions that have to be fulfilled in any small working group if it is going to be successful. Inevitably without the clothes of a particular industry upon them these functions will look rather naked, but they are the essential raw materials of leadership.

Your first aim as a leader is to make the task truly common by communicating or sharing it, that is assuming that you have been given a definite objective by your superior which the group do not know about. But that is only one type of situation, a relatively straightforward one. You may be in a group that is responsible for defining its own objectives under your leadership, or the responsibility for defining objectives may rest upon your shoulders. But what is an *objective?*

You may have noted already that *task* is a fairly general word. It means a work required by an employer or a situation. Tasks come in different shapes and sizes. They are also often gift-wrapped in misleading terms. The leader, either on his own or with others, may have to bend his analytical powers of mind to penetrate the core of the task. One vital question is to ask, 'How will we know when we have succeeded?' If that question cannot be answered it is usually a sign that the task is not yet clear enough.

You can visualise tasks in terms of differing sizes. Some people find it useful to call them by different names – *objectives, aims* and *purposes*. Others prefer to distinguish between *short-term* and *long-term objectives*. The dictionary will not help you here: our language uses such words rather loosely. It is obvious, however, that there is a difference between the broader, less defined *aim* and the more tangible or definite *objective*.

Windlesham Ltd are in the business of making bath plugs. You could call that their *purpose*. They have two *aims*: to make the best bath plugs in the world and to capture 60 per cent of the world market in the next three years (they have 35 per cent at present). Bill Jackson is just one supervisor at their Chobham factory. The *objective* this week for his section is to make 3000 one-inch plugs for a new town in Saudi-Arabia.

A familiar picture-word for objective is *target*, originally the mark at which archers shot their arrows. A target is visible. You can clearly see the arrows sticking in the outer and inner rings or the bullseye. It is certainly tangible, being made of wood, canvas and straw.

A *goal* is another such picture-word. A football match takes place within clearly-defined limits of space and time; players can see instantly if they score a goal. If they are frustrated they can go and kick the goalposts! To score goals in a match or to reach the finishing line in a marathon race calls for prolonged effort and hardship, and those overtones often colour the use of the word goal in ordinary working life. Remember that an *objective* is tangible, concrete, limited in time; an *aim* is less defined but is still fairly substantial rather than abstract; but a *purpose* may be couched in general or value terms.

The apparently quite simple behaviour of a leader telling a group what to do in fact discloses several distinct levels of ability. These cannot be directly associated with the levels of leadership, incidentally, although there ought to be some co-relation between them. These can be identified for you, along with some common mistakes to avoid (see Fig. 6.1).

Perhaps the key one for you to focus upon first is the ability to break down the *general* into the *particular*. Aristotle, who acted as mentor to the son of King Philip of Macedon – the future Alexander the Great – taught his pupil the simple lesson of how to take a general intention and turn it into a specific objective. That is why Alexander was able to conquer the known world. Unfortunately he eventually ran out of both world and time, but that is another story. All leaders need this skill of quarrying objectives out of aims, and then cutting *steps* into the objectives so that they can be achieved. Or, as the President of the World Bank put it more colourfully, 'If you are going to eat an elephant you have to do it one mouthful at a time'.

The reverse process – relating the *particular* to the *general* – is equally important. Leaders tend naturally to give *the reason why* something has to be done; bosses just tell you to do it. Answering the question 'why' means connecting it in the group's mind with the larger ongoing aims or purposes,

SUMMARY

Within the compass of the three circles, defining the task is a vital leadership function. Task is a general word. It needs to be broken down into *objectives, aims* and *purpose*. As a leader you should be able to range up and down from the particular to the general within the *task* circle. Such thinking is the necessary preliminary to *communication*. For leadership implies communicating the whys as well as the whats of work that has to be done. A good leader is a forward thinker. He

Communicating the Objective	
Abilities	Mistakes to avoid
Telling the group the objective you have been given	Not understanding it yourself first. Indistinctness or lack of clarity in briefing. 'I thought you said two inch plugs, Bill'. So check understanding.
Telling the group not only *what* to do, but also *why*	Giving the reason in terms of a past event rather than the future. 'Why are we doing it, Jack? That's simple. The boss told me to bloody well do it'. A better answer would be: 'That Saudi Arabian order is vital, Jack, if we are going to achieve our market share aim in the Middle East'.
Breaking down an aim into objectives for other groups	Not making them specific enough. Leaving parts of the aim uncovered by objectives, so that the objectives do not add up to completing the aim.
Agreeing the objective	Taking things for granted. 'Sorry we didn't complete your Saudi Arabian order, Peter. I had three other rush orders on and two machines out of action. I could have told you we couldn't do it'.
Relating aim to purpose so that you can answer the questions 'Why are we doing it; in order to achieve what?'	Confusing your department's aim with the organisation's purpose. 'Damn it, Henry, we are in business to make the world's best plugs'. 'Rubbish, Peter, the real end is to get as big a market share as possible'.

Fig. 6.1

Abilities	Mistakes to avoid
Defining purpose and checking that aims relate to it and to each other	Not doing it often enough. 'Come on, Peter and Henry, Windleshams is in business to produce a certain goods at a profit – a high quality product and a fair market share are both vital to the end. You are team members – not rivals!"
Re-defining purpose; making it more general so as to create more *aims* and *objectives*	Doing it too often. Not sensing that it has to be done. 'Since I became managing director of Windleshams a year ago it has dawned on me that we are really in the business of equipping bathrooms. Why not make the baths for our plugs?'
Communicating *purpose* to the shopfloor	Using the wrong language. Completely by-passing leaders below you. Relying solely on others to do it for you.

Fig. 6.1 (continued)

answers the question why, not with a backward-looking sentence – 'because we have always done it this way' – but with a forward-looking one – 'in order to achieve this aim or that purpose'. Clarity about the task is often difficult to achieve. But it is essential to acquire it yourself and then to share it with others.

Defining the task is not something you have to do only at the beginning of an enterprise. Confusion about the end of a task can soon invade a group or organisation. So you should be ready to define the end when the need arises.

CHECKLIST:
DEFINING THE TASK

	Yes	No
1 Are you clear about the *objectives* of your group now and for the next few years/months, and have you agreed them with your boss?	☐	☐
2 Do you fully understand the wider *aims* and *purpose* of the organisation?	☐	☐
3 Can you relate the objectives of your group to those larger, more general intentions?	☐	☐
4 Does your present main objective have sufficient specificity? Is it defined in terms of time? Is it as concrete or tangible as you can make it?	☐	☐
5 Will the group be able to know soon for themselves if you succeed or fail? Does it have swift feedback of results?	☐	☐

7 Planning

Planning is the activity of bridging the gap mentally from where you and the group are now to where you want to be at some future moment in terms of accomplishing a task. The planning function is the response to the group's need: 'How are we going to achieve the task?' But the 'how' question soon leads you to ask also 'who does what?' and 'when does it have to be done?'. Indeed, as a planner you could do worse than memorise Rudyard Kipling's short checklist:

> I keep six honest serving men
> (They taught me all I knew);
> Their names are *What* and *Why* and *When*,
> And *How* and *Where* and *Who*.

Usually if a plan proves to be inadequate, it is because either you as the leader or the group (or both) have not pressed home these questions until you have clear and definite answers.

> Calmex, a major paint company, produced a new paint stripper three times faster and more effective than the other brands on the market. John Robinson, the sales director, drew up an advertising plan to support the launch. But one agency failed to produce an important TV commercial on time. When Robinson remonstrated, the agency head got out the plan. 'It says here that you wanted it "as soon as possible". We thought next month would do.'

So planning is essentially about devising a method for making or doing something or achieving an end. A leader without plans is not likely to be effective. How do you develop skill as a planner?

SEARCHING FOR ALTERNATIVES

There is a skill in conjuring out from your own mind and from the group a sufficient number of alternative methods to choose from . Shortage of *time* obviously can limit you. If you are trying to avoid a car crash you do not have time to consider all the feasible alternatives: you have to select the first one that flashes into your mind. One of the first questions you should ask is, 'How much time have I got?' If necessary, test those time constraints to see if they are *real* as opposed to *assumed* ones. We often have more time to make a plan than we think we do. Provided there is not a crisis or an emergency and you know how much time is available, you can apply yourself to using that planning time to good effect. Keep a careful check on the time, however, because it soon goes.

Another factor you must take into account are the resources available to you in identifying the different feasible courses of action or solutions. What *people* can you consult? Your group

Sharing Decisions		
Degree of participation	Useful	Not useful
1 You present a tentative plan subject to change if another in the group comes up with a better one	When group time is short. Where you have much experience in the field and are fairly sure you are right.	Where time is plentiful and the group is as technically competent as you are. When you are only going through the motions, being unwilling to accept any changes.
2 You present the problem and get suggestions from the group	It involves the group much more than 1. Groups can be far more creative than their individual members – including you. 'Two heads are better than one'	Can be time-consuming. If group lacks sufficient knowledge and interest in the matter in hand.
3 You present a firm plan, subject to only minor changes of detail to improve it.	When you are absolutely sure that you are right. Where time is critically short.	Where the group needs to be more involved in the thinking and deciding if it is to be really committed to action

Fig. 7.1

who are going to carry out the plan are especially important. Think out the appropriate strategy for involving them on the lines of the following appreciation of the three policies.

In the positions shown in Fig. 7.1 (which you may take up in different situations during a single working day) it is assumed that you as the leader will take the decision to do it *this* way rather than *that* way at the end of the first phase of planning. Should you ever allow the group as a whole to take the decision? That depends upon what might be called the *political constitution* – written or unwritten – of the group or organisation, which usually makes these things fairly clear. Some main types of situation can be identified as shown in Fig. 7.2.

Position	Notes
You are an *elected leader, leading the group who elected you.*	The group as a whole may well wish to choose between alternative outline plans itself. It may expect you to put the matter to a vote or to test for consensus.
You are an *emergent* leader, without any formal authority at all. The group look to you for a lead.	You can influence the group to adopt one course rather than another. But, if you want to stay leader, you'll have to go along with the group choice if it contradicts your own judgement. The political constitution will be informal and often vague. Both you and the group may appeal to precedents in decision making.
You are an *appointed* leader, with a clearly defined authority	If you are ultimately accountable for the work of the group, you can justly claim to have the last word on the decision.

Fig. 7.2

As you will see, there are some 'grey areas' in sharing decision-making with a group. You may be two if not all three of these types of leader. The Prime Minister, for example, is emergent, elected and appointed. Even if you have the authority to propose your own plan and carry it out, or arbitrarily to choose among the several possibilities put forward the one that you like best personally, you may be reluctant to use that authority, for you want to involve and commit the group. There is a commonsense principle that the more a group (or individual) shares in the thinking and decision making process the more it is likely to be committed to making the agreed plan work. But keep a firm control of the process.

In groups where all members are roughly equal in competence the choice between alternatives may be debated hotly. Leaders as well as members need to be able to put the case for a course of action as persuasively as they can, while remaining open-minded and honest enough to recognise the truth when it emerges from any quarter. Such a process belongs to the essence of democracy. 'Whenever men can be persuaded rather than ordered – when they can be made to feel that they have participated in developing the plan – they

---

On planning

Chris Bonnington is internationally famous as a leader of mountaineering expeditions. In this letter he sets out his strategy for involving the group fully:

'At the planning stage of an expedition I get as close consultation and involvement of all members of the team as possible. I do this by a series of meetings and discuss in full each step of the expedition gaining consensus agreement on every aspect of the trip. This is extremely important since it gives me, the leader, a clear rider for pursuing a course of action on the mountain which has already been agreed upon. It also ensures that everyone is in agreement on both the organisation and methods used to put the expedition together and, in addition, of course, on the money side of things. The deeper the involvement of individual members the greater their commitment and also enthusiasm. At this stage I feel my role is that of the chairman of a committee. If I go into each meeting with a clearly thought out plan which I present to my fellow team members in a positive and well reasoned way, the probability is that the plan will be adopted. On the other hand, there might be areas for improvement and I think it is important that whoever is chairing such a meeting is prepared to adopt any worthwhile suggestions. The important thing is that he does maintain his dominance of the meeting and doesn't let it develop into a messy discussion.

This really goes on into the expedition itself. Once on the mountain I keep a very close eye and feel on the consensus opinion of the team. On a climbing expedition it is impossible to steamroll the group into doing something they don't really want to do. At the same time, I try to avoid too many discursive meetings, making my main strategic decisions myself, after, perhaps, informal discussions with some members of the team. The vital thing is to be right for most of the time. One can achieve this by putting a great deal of thought into each step.'

Chris Bonnington

approach their tasks with understanding and enthusiasm', said Eisenhower. He recalled that Churchill was a persuader during the planning phase.

> Indeed his skill in the use of words and logic was so great that on several occasions when he and I disagreed on some important matter – even when I was convinced of the correctness of my own view and when the responsibility was clearly mine – I had a very hard time withstanding his arguments. More than once he forced me to re-examine my own premises, to convince myself again that I was right – or accept his solution. Yet if the decision went against him, he accepted it with good grace, and did everything in his power to support it with proper action. Leadership by persuasion and the wholehearted acceptance of a contrary decision are both fundamentals of democracy.

It becomes clear that without leadership any form of democracy can be inert and feeble. When all people can feel themselves to be equal in value, if not in knowledge and experience, that is the beginning of true leadership – not its end. As Montesquieu wrote, 'To suggest where you cannot compel, to guide where you cannot demand, that is the supreme form of skill'.

HOW TO BE MORE CREATIVE

Planning doesn't sound very creative, does it? All those typed schedules and drawings or diagrams. But a plan grows from an idea. That idea is the germ of a method, solution or course. Perhaps the most common mistake is to make an *unconscious assumption* which limits the number or kind of methods. 'It is quite clear', a personnel manager announced to his staff recently, 'that we can do only two things about Bill Jackson in accounts: move him sideways or sack him. Which will it be?'

The better leaders have always resisted this binary thinking – black or white, this or that. But many managers (and academics) do think in terms of either-or, because it offers a spurious clarity. This is an important stage in some cases (e.g. a judge summing up for a jury) to reduce the judgment to an issue (either this or that) if it can be done. But it is fatal to do it too quickly, so that you totally ignore the third, fourth or fifth possibilities which might have included the best suggestions. So you should make sure that you or your group generate enough options. As Bismarck used to say to his generals, 'If you think the enemy has only two courses open to him you can be sure that he will choose the third!'

> Alfred P. Sloan, when President of General Motors, is reported to have said at a meeting of one of his top committees: 'Gentlemen, I take it we are all in complete agreement on the decision here'. Everyone around the table nodded assent. 'Then', continued Sloan, 'I propose we postpone further discussion of this matter until our next meeting to give ourselves time to develop disagreement and perhaps gain some understanding of what the decision is all about'.

In most situations the three or four feasible alternatives can be identified by straightforward observation, thought and group discussion. But there is often a creative solution, so called because it is hidden until someone actually discovers it. 'How obvious and simple. Why didn't we think of that?' If they are not already familiar to you the next two exercises will make the point.

EXERCISE 9

1 Connect up the nine dots with four consecutive straight lines, i.e. without taking your pencil off the paper.

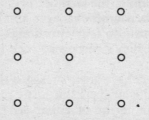

2 Take six matchsticks and put them on a table in front of you. Now arrange them into a pattern of four equilateral (equal sided) triangles, without breaking the matches. There are at least two acceptable solutions.

Now turn to p. 205 for the answers.

Karl Dunckner, the psychologist who invented the match-sticks problem in the 1920s, made the point that we develop *functional fixedness* as we grow older. For us a hammer is for knocking in nails. The first step towards greater creativity is to try to free ourselves from such assumptions, useful though they are in everyday life.

EXERCISE 10

List 25 uses for a hammer other than knocking in nails or wrenching them out. You have five minutes.

You may find it hard to think of new ideas or to generate them from other people if you have picked up the habit of instant criticism.

Negative criticism directed at your own ideas or someone else's will destroy them. The technique known as 'brainstorming' works by encouraging people deliberately to *suspend judgement* – to refrain from criticism and to produce as many ideas as possible. On the other hand, if you want to stifle creative thinking here are some useful phrases for you:

That will never work.
Don't waste my time with such rubbish.
We have tried it before.
If you thought it up it must be wrong.

The concept of group climate is important here. Some groups are like a white frost on an April morning: they kill off the blossoms of ideas which might one day fruit into plans. The atmosphere is negative, hypercritical and anxious. Other groups are like warm mornings in May: positive, encouraging and confident. Leadership is a key factor in turning a negative group into a positive one. One important skill is asking leading questions, as shown in Fig. 7.3.

Each of us has 10,000 million brain cells and they are probably the most expensive resource your organisation hires. In order to secure the best quality plan you will need to involve the group's brain cells as well as your own. It pays off a high dividend in commitment.

Quality Circles originated in Japan and from 20 Circles in 1961 a staggering 10 million workers were members of Circles by 1980! Little wonder then that it has been predicted that by the end of the 1980s Japan would seize world leadership in quality.

Other countries adopting Quality Circle ideas include South Korea, Taiwan, Singapore, Brazil, Sweden, Norway, USA and Holland. Since 1975 organisations in the USA have set up about 2000 Circles. Although the figures for the UK are not known precisely they were believed to be not less than 100 by 1980.

So, what are Quality Circles?

A volunteer group of employees from the same workplace who, with their supervisor or shift leader, meet for about one hour every week in company time to discuss work problems, investigate their causes and recommend solutions. These solutions are then implemented directly or presented to management for agreement on action.

The background features of successful Circle operation include *training in leadership* and the *stimulation of creativity* by

Some Skills in Generating Ideas	
Questions/Statements	Notes
Bringing in 'Bob, you have had experience in several other industries, how did they tackle this problem?'	Meets individual needs as well as the task.
Stimulating 'Imagine we were starting from scratch again. How would we do it?'	Brains are like car engines. They need warming up by outrageous ideas or thought provoking suggestions.
Building on 'Can't we develop the idea behind Mary's suggestion of cutting down the number of files? Could we use the computer more? How else can we improve our information storage system?	Entails seeing the positive idea or principle in a suggestion and taking it one step further.
Spreading 'We can also include Jim's suggestion about time-keeping and Jack's point about safety in the plan'	Helps to develop a team solution. A creative process of weaving separate threads and loose ends together into a whole
Accepting while rejecting 'Mike's proposal is an interesting and helpful one, but it would take us rather too long so we must leave it on one side for the present'	You are accepting Mike, but rejecting his plan in a gracious way. He will not be resentful, and may come up with the winning idea next time.

Fig. 7.3

such techniques as 'brainstorming' (e.g. thinking up 20 uses of objects; free association of ideas).[1]

MAKING A CONTINGENCY PLAN

Constructing a work programme and a time plan follows naturally from the choice of a method to achieve the task. Depending on the technology involved that work programme can vary enormously in size and complexity. The only general guidance that can be given is to keep it *as simple as possible*. But there is one aspect of planning which experienced leaders tend to devote more attention to than others – contingency planning.

No one can ever make a perfect plan. You cannot foresee every eventuality. Once thinking stops and committed action begins – the real 'point-of-no-return' in decision making – there are bound to be some contingencies – things that happen by chance or through unforeseen causes which affect what you are doing. A good plan will make some provision for the contingent in human affairs. A prudent householder usually keeps a bit of money in reserve in case some of the things that are liable to happen actually do so. A wise general also keeps a reserve corps available in case the enemy does something he had not expected. So you should build a certain amount of flexibility into your plan so that you are not caught out by unforeseen (but not improbable) happenings. To repeat the point, a good leader thinks ahead. He uses his imagination in a disciplined way to picture those contingencies. His imagination is his own mental radar set. Once a possible contingency has been picked up he must estimate the chances of it occurring and make provision accordingly. Thus, you have to become an educated guesser. 'All the business of war, and indeed all the business of life', said the Duke of Wellington, is to endeavour to find out what you don't know by what you do. That's what I called guessing what was at the other side of the hill'. In the language of leadership qualities it is known as *foresight* – seeing what others cannot see because they are not tall enough to look over the hill.

SUMMARY

Planning is a key activity in any working group or organisation, and it constitutes one of the principles of leadership.

Once the task has been defined the first step in planning is to search for alternatives. More often than not this work is best done in consultation with others. It is important to not only remain open, but indeed to actively encourage, new ideas or possibilities. You should aim to become a *creative thinker* yourself and learn how to stimulate creative or innovative ideas in the group and in each individual. The example given, the recently introduced Quality Circles, is only a formalised version of what should be a natural process. But it shows that this approach of getting ideas from the group pays dividends. No plan, however original, is perfect. Always plan for foreseeable contingencies. Thus, as a planner, you should be developing the necessary abilities for sharing decision making where feasible, creative imagination and foresight. To these should be added, of course, the necessary professional knowledge and technical skills required in your particular work.

CHECKLIST:
PLANNING YOUR WORK

	Yes	No
Have you called upon specialist advice before making your plan?	☐	☐
Did you consider all the feasible courses of action and weigh them up in terms of resources needed/available and outcomes?	☐	☐
Have you a programme now which will achieve your objective?	☐	☐
Is there a provision for contingencies?	☐	☐
Did you and the group actively search for a more creative solution as the basis for your plan?	☐	☐
Have you made the plan as simple and as foolproof as possible, rather than complicated?	☐	☐
Does the plan include any necessary preparation or training of the group or individuals?	☐	☐

8 Briefing

The pilots and aircrew shuffle in their chairs and talk among themselves. Outside the rain beats down on the large Nissen hut that serves as a conference room. At 10.00 hours promptly the adjutant calls the room to attention and General Savage strides in and takes his position in the centre of the low platform, feet apart and facing the audience. 'There will be a practice mission this morning. That's right – practice. Our strike photographs show that we haven't been hitting the target lately'.

Many thousands of managers who have seen the film *Twelve O'Clock High* in the context of their ACL courses will recall this first meeting of the 918 Bomb Group called by their new commanding officer. Such briefing sessions are held in all kinds of other organisations, albeit without the drama of a wartime situation. In them the leader is performing a basic leadership function – *briefing or instructing his team*. He is instructing or informing them thoroughly in advance.

The *content* of such a briefing session is the result of carrying out two previous functions: *defining the task and planning*. After stating the objectives and why they are important you have to describe the plan – in outline first and then in greater detail (although this second activity can be delegated to a subordinate or colleague, as General Savage does in the film). It is essential for you to answer the question which will be in everyone's minds, 'What is my part going to be?' So ask yourself before and after such a briefing meeting questions such as:

Does everyone know exactly what his job is?
Has each member of the group clearly defined targets and performance standards agreed between him and me?

For the main purpose of a briefing meeting is to allocate tasks to groups and individuals, to distribute resources and to set or check standards of performance. Each person should know at the end what is expected of him and how the contribution of his sub-group or he himself fits in with the purposeful work of everyone else.

EFFECTIVE SPEAKING

A consideration of the leader's method brings us to what are sometimes called vaguely *communication skills*. Here obviously you are faced with the need to master the specific ability to speak effectively. How do you do it?

To begin with the good news, you do not have to become a great orator. You should not concern yourself with the tricks of rhetoric, the techniques taught to would-be demagogues in ancient Athens. The only test is whether or not you can speak in such a way that you *move the group to the desired action*. Demosthenes said to a rival orator: 'You make the audience say "How well he speaks!" I make them say "Let us march against Philip!" '

An element of persuasion in the sense of explaining why in a convincing way will enter into most briefing or communicating meetings. But it will happen more naturally if you have mastered the skills of speaking or briefing. We can identify five sets of skills involved in briefing a group effectively for action. In Fig. 8.1 these skills are set out, together with some examples of how to do it.

BRIEFING AND GROUP WORK

Briefing sessions or conferences – work meetings – allow you to do some valuable work in all three circles, moving general points connected with the specific matter in hand. In the task area, for example, you can make it the occasion (as General Savage did) for taking charge. A certain amount of assertiveness is often required of leaders and the group will accept it – even welcome it – if the situation calls for it. You can stress the team approach to the task in hand, thus building up team spirit. You can meet *individual* needs by listening to and acknowledging the help of those who help you to achieve the ends of the meeting. It can also be an opportunity for emphasising the significance of each individual's contribution to the success of the enterprise.

General Savage in the film was using the medium of the briefing session to convey or share his vision, standards or

Briefing Skills		
Skill	Definition	How you can do it
Preparing	The ability to think ahead and plan your communication	Give a beginning, middle and end in your talk. Prepare good visual aids, not too many. Arrange the room in advance.
Clarifying	The ability to make clear or understandable	Unravel the difficulties in your own mind first. Avoid obscure ways of putting things. Seek clarifying questions.
Simplifying	The ability to render complex matters into their simple forms	Relating the unfamiliar to the familiar by homely analogies. Avoid complicated terminology. Give an overview or outline first. Summarise.
Vivifying	The ability to make a subject come alive	Use of vivid language or methods, even gimmicks. Be enthusiastic and aim to enthuse the group. Use humour if possible.
Being yourself	The ability to cope with nerves and to behave naturally in front of an audience	Breathe deeply. Eliminate nervous habits. Bear yourself well.

Fig. 8.1

values. Some of the supreme examples of leadership occur when a leader takes over a demoralised group and 'turns it around'. The initial briefing meeting can be especially important in this process. For first impressions are as basic in working relationships as in love and friendship. The impression you make on people at that first meeting will stay with them for ever. The task may have to be covered in general terms if you are new to the job – you can do little more than share your first thoughts. But you can share your vision, your spirit of resolve and your determination to change the climate and standards of the group. That may require some tough talking, and people will wait to see if it is going to be backed up by equally firm deeds.

Read this case study in the art of briefing, and then work on the questions at the end.

On 13th August 1942 Montgomery arrived at Eighth Army Headquarters, two months before the battle of Alamein. 'The atmosphere was dismal and dreary', he wrote in his diary. That evening he addressed the entire staff of Army Headquarters, between fifty and sixty officers. As he was their fourth Army Commander within a year, he faced a sceptical audience. They plainly doubted if he was the man to reverse their recent defeats and failures. If the morale of that broken army was to be recreated their hearts had to be won that evening.

Montgomery stood on the steps of his predecessor's caravan and bade the gathering sit on the sand. He spoke without notes, looking straight at his audience.

'I want first of all to introduce myself to you. You do not know me. I do not know you. But we have got to work together; therefore we must understand each other and we must have confidence in each other. I have only been here a few hours. But from what I have seen and heard since I arrived I am prepared to say, here and now, that I have confidence in you. We will then work together as a team; and together we will gain the confidence of this great army and go forward to final victory in Africa.

I believe that one of the first duties of a commander is to create what I call, 'atmosphere' and in that atmosphere, his staff, subordinate commanders and troops will live and work and fight.

I do not like the general atmosphere I find here. It is an

atmosphere of doubt, of looking back to select the next place
to which to withdraw, of loss of confidence in our ability to
defeat Rommel, of desperate defence measures by reserves in
preparing positions in Cairo and the Delta. All that must
cease. Let us have a new atmosphere.

The defence of Egypt lies here in Alamein and on the
Ruweisat Ridge. What is the use of digging trenches in the
Delta? It is quite useless; if we lose this position we lose Egypt;
all the fighting troops now in the Delta must come here at
once, and will. Here we will stand and fight; there will be no
further withdrawal. I have ordered that all plans and instructions dealing with further withdrawal are to be burnt at once.
We will stand and fight here.

If we can't stay here alive, then let us stay here dead.

I want to impress on everyone that the bad times are over.
Fresh divisions from the UK are now arriving in Egypt, together with ample reinforcements for our present divisions.
We have 300 to 400 Sherman new tanks coming and these are
actually being unloaded at Suez now. Our mandate from the
Prime Minister is to destroy the Axis forces in North Africa;
I have seen it written on half a sheet of notepaper. And it will
be done. If anyone here thinks it can't be done, let him go at
once; I don't want any doubters in this party. It can be done,
and it will be done; beyond any possibility of doubt.

Now I understand that Rommel is expected to attack at any
moment. Excellent. Let him attack.

I would sooner it didn't come for a week, just to give me
time to sort things out. If we have two weeks to prepare we
will be sitting pretty; Rommel can attack as soon as he likes
after that, and I hope he does.

Meanwhile, we ourselves will start to plan a great offensive;
it will be the beginning of a campaign which will hit Rommel
and his army for six right out of Africa.

But first we must create a reserve corps, mobile and strong
in armour which we will train out of the line. Rommel has
always had such a force in his Afrika Corps, which is never
used to hold the line but which is always in reserve available
for striking blows. Therein has been his great strength. We
will create such a corps ourselves, a British Panzer Corps; it
will consist of two armoured divisions and one motorised division; I gave orders yesterday for it to begin to form, back in
the Delta.

I have no intention of launching our great attack until we
are completely ready. There will be pressure from many quarters to attack soon; I will not attack until we are ready and
you can rest assured on that point.

Meanwhile, if Rommel attacks while we are preparing let him do so with pleasure; we will merely continue with our own preparations and we will attack when we are ready and not before.

I want to tell you that I always work on the chief-of-staff system. I have nominated Brigadier de Guingand as chief-of-staff Eighth Army. I will issue orders through him. Whatever he says will be taken as coming from me and will be acted on at once. I understand there has been a great deal of 'belly-aching' out here. By 'belly-aching' I mean inventing poor reasons for not doing what one has been told to do.

All this is to stop at once.

I will tolerate no belly-aching. If anyone objects to doing what he is told, then he can get out of it; and at once. I want that made very clear right down through the Eighth Army.

I have little more to say just at present. And some of you may think it is quite enough and may wonder if I am mad. I assure you I am quite sane.

I understand there are people who often think I am slightly mad; so often that I now regard it as rather a compliment.

All I have to say to that is that if I am slightly mad, there are a large number of people I could name who are raving lunatics.

What I have done is to get over to you the 'atmosphere' in which we will now work and fight; you must see that that atmosphere permeates right down through the Eighth Army to the most junior private soldier. All the soldiers must know what is wanted; when they see it coming to pass there will be a surge of confidence throughout the army.

I ask you to give me your confidence and to have faith that what I have said will come to pass.

There is much work to be done. The orders I have given about no further withdrawal will mean a complete change in the layout of our dispositions; also that we must begin to prepare for our great offensive.

The first thing to do is to move our HQ to a decent place where we can live in reasonable comfort and where the army staff can all be together and side by side with the HQ of the Desert Air Force. This is a frightful place here, depressing, unhealthy and a rendezvous for every fly in Africa; we shall do no good work here. Let us get over there by the sea where it is fresh and healthy. If officers are to do good work they must have decent messes, and be comfortable. So off we go on the new line.

The chief-of-staff will be issuing orders on many points very shortly, and I am always available to be consulted by the senior officers of the staff. The great point to remember is that we are going to finish with this chap Rommel once and for all. It will be quite easy. There is no doubt about it.

He is definitely a nuisance. Therefore we will hit him a crack and finish with him.[1]

Montgomery stepped down and the officers rose and stood to attention. 'One could have heard a pin drop if such a thing were possible in the sand of the desert', recollected Montgomery. 'But it certainly had a profound effect, and a spirit of hope, anyway of clarity, was born that evening'. His chief-of-staff, de Guingand, agreed: 'It was one of his greatest efforts,' he wrote, 'The effect of the address was electric – it was terrific! And we all went to bed that night with new hope in our hearts, and a great confidence in the future of our Army. I wish someone had taken it down in shorthand, for it would have become a classic of its kind.' Fortunately, it *was* taken down in shorthand and filed away for many years before appearing in print for the first time in 1981.

EXERCISE 11

1 How did Montgomery set about changing the group atmosphere?
2 What was the common objective he communicated?
3 What was the new outline plan?
4 Did he set any new group standards?
5 What did he expect from all present?
6 How did he respond to the individual needs of the staff?
7 If you had to choose one word to summarise Montgomery's message, what would it be?

In 1981 the new Chairman of British Steel, Ian Macgregor, talked about 'holding the Alamein line' to his managers. The industry had been hard hit by recession, with many plant closures and massive redundancies. Confidence in the future of British Steel was flagging. It was still losing a million pounds a day. But the Chairman had identified a viable set of plants and could announce that there would be no further 'retreat' beyond that new profile.

Attitudes among managers and trade unions have begun to change. Although the situations of the Eighth Army in 1942 and British Steel in 1981 were not exactly comparable (despite the presence of some German and Italian competition!) you can see why and how top leaders always need to perform the vital function of *briefing* their immediate group.

BRIEFING THE ORGANISATION

Senior leaders should be able to rely upon their immediate subordinates (line and function/staff leaders) to relay the message down the line. Some industrial organisations have set up systems known as briefing groups to ensure that this happens. But in addition a senior leader should make time to talk directly to employees.

> Summer before last at the Rowntree chocolate factory in York, I listened to one of the best speeches I have ever heard. When a group of new girls is taken into this factory—they take in thirty at a time—Mr. Rowntree, the president, gives a talk to these girls. He tells them what their work is all about, he shows them how one person being careless in dipping chocolates may make the young man who takes a box of chocolates to his best girl on Saturday night say that he won't get Rowntree's chocolates next time. And then Mr. Rowntree shows how this affects far more than Rowntree profits, how in time reduced sales will mean less employment in York for girls and boys, for men and women. And then he goes on, from such simple illustrations, to show them their place in the industry of England. I don't believe it is possible for those who hear these talks not to feel a close connection with, a certain degree of identification with, the Rowntree Company. While leadership depends on depth of conviction and the power coming therefrom, there must also be the ability to share that conviction with others. Mr. Rowntree, by his vivid statement of purpose, has found a way of making all his employees share in a common purpose.[2]

The outstanding leaders of the Second World War – Eisenhower, Slim, Montgomery and Mountbatten – all practised this direct approach. They were not too busy. As young men they had suffered in the First World War under generals who never came near the front line or left their comfortable headquarters in order to tell the subalterns and men *what* was going to happen and *why* it was important. So they resolved that if ever they rose to command armies in war they would perform the briefing function. In the Arab Legion I served under Lieutenant-General Sir John Glubb, who had also been a subaltern in the First World War. Among the vivid recollections I have of him are his visits, when he would sit informally with groups of officers and soldiers, briefing them on the situation.

Glubb Pasha at work

Considering the blessings which can result from human comradeship, we come to a subject on which I feel strongly – the ever increasing bureaucracy and the endless hours spent at a desk. The office tends to overshadow the whole of life, making leadership and human relationships increasingly difficult. This unfortunate tendency is felt in every department of life, whether it be administration, the armed services, industry, the chuch or any other activity.

Paperwork makes human relations weaker. Instead of leading his subordinates, the senior man spends all his day at his desk. Moreover the office becomes a routine to which a man becomes so accustomed that he finds it more and more difficult to get out and about.

Personally I found this office life so insidious that I often felt myself obliged to establish my own rules and to compel myself to adhere to them. For example, I would decide to spend three days a week in the office and three days visiting the men at their work, or in the field. On days when I was out, a summary of the office work could be sent round to my house after office hours.

Our satisfaction in our work also depends on our knowledge of its value and utility. When commanding the Arab Legion in Jordan, I tried, as often as possible, to address all ranks and to explain to them the general situation and what we were trying to do. In military service, of course, there may be certain subjects which must be kept secret. But we found a wide area of information, which was not secret, but which the private soldier would not discover unless it were brought to his notice. This sharing of information with subordinates creates a sense of partnership which consolidates the whole organisation into a single team.

The happiest times of my life were passed in junior positions, as a company commander in the British Army, or with the hundred-man Desert Patrol in Trans-Jordan in the 1930s. In such junior posts it is possible to know every man intimately, his family and his background. Often, in those days, I was able to help these men in their private affairs, to arrange for the admission of their wives and children to hospital, to obtain legal advice in their troubles or to help them in other ways.

Unfortunately promotion to higher posts makes it impossible to know everybody and severs many familiar relationships. Yet even managers of senior commanders can frequently visit their men at work, address them on subjects of interest to them and encourage the junior officers to take a personal interest in them.

One of the beneficial results of constantly visiting subordinates is the ability to know as many people as possible, to recognize them, remember their names and their personal circumstances.

> In the course of these addresses or conversations, it is possible to tell them of the objects of the work, to inform them of the successes achieved, of tributes paid to us in the press or by outside individuals and of our superiority over other similar units or groups. By this means, it is possible to rouse in them a pride in the organization to which they belong and in their own contribution to its success.
>
> Another essential aspect of leadership is to remember to thank and to praise those who do well. So many senior men are ready instantly to pounce on a fault, but remain silent when all is going well. Every senior man should always remember to praise, where praise is due.
>
> *Lieut. General Sir John Glubb*
> *Arabian Adventures, Cassell, 1978*

BRIEFING THE INDIVIDUAL

Briefing individuals – giving instructions – is a perennial function of leadership. Like all functions it can be done well, in which case it becomes a skill; or it can be done badly, in which case it is called a disaster. In a crisis or an emergency, those instructions are usually given as commands or orders. Where that life-or-death element or obvious shortage of time is not there it is best to give instructions in the form of suggestions or questions. Where possible give reasons for the action.

> Tony, I suggest you get that report about sales in France into the marketing director by next Friday, not the following Tuesday. I know he needs it for a Board meeting on Monday. Could you do that, please?

From an early age I noticed that I tended to do things much more willingly if my parents or teachers *asked* me nicely, rather than told me. That may be a personal idiosyncrasy, or an English one. My impression, however, is that most people react in the same way. That is why an element of natural courtesy should flavour all that a leader does. Certainly I have noticed that good leaders tend to ask you to do things – they do not boss you about.

Clearly, performing the briefing function with understanding and skill takes you well beyond the specific example of

---

A Short Course on Leadership

The six most important words...

"I admit I made a mistake."
The five most important words...
"I am proud of you."
The four most important words...
"What is your opinion?"

The three most important words...

"If you please."
The two most important words...
"Thank you"
The one most important word...
"We."

And the least most important word...

"I".

---

giving instructions to your team before tackling an objective. In this wider context it involves a sustained attempt in the group or organisation to let people know what is going on and to create or build a spirit of positive, constructive and confident teamwork.

SUMMARY

Perhaps the word most closely associated with leadership in people's minds is *communication*. A good leader communicates. But it is important for you to become more specific than that. In this chapter we have looked at the *briefing* function. That apparently simple activity does call for a number of skills that can be developed.

At the first level of leadership you should strive to become competent at briefing your group on objectives and plans. At the senior level you will have to brief the organisation, a much more demanding task. At all levels there are individuals who need to be briefed in clear and simple language. Such occasions – group, organisational or individual – are not to be seen merely in terms of the task. They are also opportunities for you to create the right *atmosphere*, to promote *teamwork*, and to get to know, encourage and motivate each *individual* person.

CHECKLIST:
BRIEFING

Do you regularly brief your group on the organisation's current plans and future developments?

Yes ☐   No ☐

How would you rate yourself on each of five skills of briefing effectively:

	Good	Adequate	Weak
Preparing			
Clarifying			
Simplifying			
Vivifying			
Being yourself			

In what specific ways can you improve your skills?

(1)

(2)

(3)

Can you identify the most effective briefing talk by a senior manager that you have ever heard? In one sentence, why was it effective?

Could your organisation improve its two-way communication of information and instructions with those responsible for carrying them out?

Yes ☐   No ☐

9 Controlling

'No one will miss this bag of gold if I slip it under the table. In the account I'll put it down as travel expenses.'

In the Middle Ages the royal servants in the various departments of state were not above helping themselves from the till. Hence, it was necessary to supervise their accounts of payments and receipts by keeping a duplicate roll. Then you could check or verify payments *contra rotulus*, against that second roll. This medieval invention has given us our modern word *control*. In its wider sense, controlling means checking and directing action once work has started to implement the plan.

At the outset you have to establish that you are in charge. Then you have to maintain that control. Again, that does not mean that you will do all the leadership work yourself. But in their eagerness to help there is always a danger that a sub-group or an individual member will in effect take over control from you. Such specialists or strong individuals can be given their head on occasion, but you should keep the reins firmly in your own hands. However quiet you may be by nature, you must not allow anyone to dominate you or the group. Brave self-assertion is needed. Timidity is out. It is fatal to authority if you give instructions (as orders, suggestions or questions) and feel like a small boy who throws a stone and runs away.

Once work has started on a project it is vitally important that you supervise or monitor what is being done, so that everyone's energy is turning wheels – or most of it anyway, for humans are as inefficient as old steam engines and steam is always escaping in one way or another. But most of that synergy or common energy of the group should be fully deployed in the common plan.

How do you do it? The secret of controlling is to have a clear idea in your mind what should be happening, when it should occur, who should be doing it and how it should be done. The more effectively you have involved the group in your planning the more likely it is that they too will have a similar clear picture of what is required. The ideal is that the group or the individual with whom you are dealing should become self-controlling, so as to regulate its own performance against standards or the clock. 'We have only got two hours left, and so we shall have to work harder to get the job done to meet the deadline.' Your aim as a leader is to intervene as little as possible.

Keeping a low profile

A leader is best
When people barely know that he exists.
Not so good when people obey and acclaim him,
Worst when they despise him.
'Fail to honour people,
They fail to honour you';
But of a good leader, who talks little,
When his work is done, his aim fulfilled,
They will all say, 'We did this ourselves.'

Lao-Tzu
6th Century B.C.

Your object, then, in directing, regulating and restraining is to ensure that the group's work keeps within bounds or on course. That is the sole criterion of your effectiveness as a controller. You have oversight, which means you should be able to look at the whole picture. If problems crop up, such as obstacles or difficulties, in the path of the adopted course you are then in a good position to help the group to cope with them.

The stance of a controller is to be where the action is, but observing rather than doing. If you watch a good leader in the execution phase of an exercise or project, his eyes are never still. The pattern of ability here is: 1 observe; 2 think; 3 intervene. Obviously if a safety standard is being ignored and someone is in danger of losing life or limb, your thought processes will be instant. But much of what you see will be below standard or performance (especially if you are inclined to be a perfectionist) and you will have to make a judgement whether or not to intervene.

If you decide on intervention, the principle is to use the minimum force possible. If you imagine that you are at the controls of an ocean racing yacht, you do not normally have to yank the rudder about or lunge around with a boathook. In order to get the group onto its agreed course again you may only have to touch the controls – a quiet word or even a look can do the trick. The personal course you have to steer as a leader should take you between the two black rocks of *too much interference* and *lack of direction*. Many a leader is shipwrecked in these foaming straits.

If the plan is going well and the group is composed of self-disciplining people, you can sometimes have time to help an individual or a sub-group with their part of the task. If you want everyone to work hard you must not give the impression that you are standing around with nothing to do. Yet you should always remain in such a position that you can instantly take control if things begin to go wrong. Some leaders make the mistake of getting so involved in a piece of work that they forget their responsibility for the whole. You do not see the whole forest if you are busy cutting down a tree – which your woodman could do better than you if only he could get his hands on *his* axe! Setting an example of hard work is always a good idea, as long as it does not detract from your function as director and controller.

CONTROLLING A MEETING

Taking the chair in committees and at meetings is a leadership role. Therefore the model of the three-circles applies. Decision making is essential too, because that is usually what meetings and committees are about. Consequently there is relatively little to be added specifically about the chairman's job providing you have grasped the elements of good leadership. What matters most then is to observe and learn from experienced chairmen at work. They are rare people, and you should not miss the opportunity of watching closely how they conduct a meeting so that the tasks are achieved, the group works as a team and each individual contributes effectively according to their talents.

There are some leadership functions needed more frequently in committees and meetings than elsewhere. The skill of silencing people in a firm but friendly way has to be developed. The skill of testing for consensus is also vital. A good chairman will sense that area of consensus, which is rather like the invisible ever-moving centre of a shoal of fish. Here his ability to read non-verbal behaviour – a raised eyebrow, a half-smile, a vigorous nod – can be significant. If you watch a good leader in the chair you will notice that he always keeps an eye upon the faces of the committee members. Lastly, the skill of summarising may have to be employed more than once during a meeting. It is a means of taking bearings, to ensure that the ship is still on course.

Controlling the Cabinet

The Cabinet usually meets once a week. That should be enough for regular meetings, and should be if they grasp from the start what they are there for. They should be back at their work as soon as possible, and a Prime Minister should put as little as possible in their way. We started sharp at 11, and rose in time for lunch. Even in a crisis, another couple of meetings should be enough in the same week: if there is a crisis, the less talk the better.

The Prime Minister shouldn't speak too much himself in Cabinet. He should start the show or ask somebody else to do so, and then intervene only to bring out the more modest chaps who, despite their seniority, might say nothing if not asked. And the Prime Minister must sum up. Experienced Labour leaders should be pretty good at this; they have spent years attending debates at meetings of the Parliamentary Party and the National Executive, and have to sum *those* up. That takes some doing – good training for the Cabinet.

Particularly when a non-Cabinet Minister is asked to attend, especially if it is his first time, the Prime Minister may have to be cruel. The visitor may want to show how good he is, and go on too long. A good thing is to take no chance and ask him to send the Cabinet a paper in advance. The Prime Minister can then say, 'A very clear statement, Minister. Do you need to add anything?' in a firm tone of voice obviously expecting the answer, *No*. If somebody else looks like making a speech, it is sound to nip in with 'Has anybody any objection?' If somebody starts to ramble, a quick, 'Are you *objecting*? You're not? Right. Next business,' and the Cabinet can move on.

It is essential for the Cabinet to move on, leaving in its wake a trail of clear, crisp, uncompromising decisions. This is what government is about. And the challenge to democracy is how to get it done quickly.

Clement Attlee

CONTROLLING IN ORGANISATIONS

In organisations as opposed to groups it is essential that some *control systems* are established, for a leader at the top cannot obviously do all the controlling himself. What he has to do in concert with the senior leadership team is to ensure that leaders at all levels are carrying out the controlling function. In order to control, the controlling system of checks has to be introduced to give him the necessary information. Successful industrial organisations are characterised by both delegation of the controlling function right down to the shopfloor and also by some strategic financial controls.

Rolleron Ltd, a firm making garden tools and machinery, really took off in 1976 when it bought Clive Mitchell's invention of a lawn-mower capable of self-sharpening. The machine was also especially resistant to stones damaging the blades and throwing them out of true. By 1980 the firm had grown from 300 to 3000 employees. But the top leadership failed to introduce a proper system of annual budgeting, with monthly checks against the target figures. Costs rose; debts mounted. The company's board did not receive information in time of a slight down-swing in the lawn-mower market, which would have allowed them to switch resources to other areas. A cash flow problem proved to be the straw which broke the camel's back in 1981. 'A company with an excellent product and willing staff', said the public receiver in his report on its bankruptcy. 'But its management failed to establish proper financial controls'.

That story is by no means unique. A similar defect caused the crash of Rolls Royce Ltd in 1971. The one characteristic that almost all companies that fail possess is poor two-way communication in the controlling function. At whatever level you are operating as a leader you have to direct and control the situation – or it will control you.

SELF-CONTROL

If you cannot control yourself you are unlikely to be able to control others. Take bad temper as an example. An occasional explosion of anger does no harm if the provocation is evident and great. Leaders are not placid, and the capacity for justified anger is important. But bad temper is a different matter. It is far from being a harmless weakness, a mere matter of temperament. If you are easily ruffled, quick-tempered or 'touchy' by disposition, people will diagnose it as caused by a lack of patience, kindness, courtesy or unselfishness.

Remember, however, that all your weaknesses are merely tendencies to act in a certain way. They do not guarantee that you will do so. Hundreds of leaders have successfully curbed their fiery tempers, harnessing the energy released rather than allowing it to simply 'blow their top'. 'Leaders,' said St. Paul, 'should not be "easily provoked".'

There are plenty of other aspects in us that invite self-control. Just controlling your tongue – that unruly member – can be a formidable job. The encouraging fact is that each small victory over one of these tendencies makes the next encounter a little easier. As Shakespeare wrote,

> Refrain tonight,
> And that shall lend a kind of easiness
> To the next abstinence, the next more easy;
> For use almost can change the stamp of nature.

There are some situations which naturally invite fear or anxiety. Everyone must be aware that fear is contagious. An animal can smell or sense whether or not you are afraid of it, so can people. You only have to recollect how panic can suddenly seize a crowd without a word being spoken. But courage – the resource in us which enables us to contain or overcome fear – is also contagious.

Being human you will have as much fear and anxiety as anyone else in the group or organisation. But fear paralyses. If you want the group to continue working then fear has to be neutralised. If you can calm yourself, remaining a still centre in the storm, that calmness will be radiated to others. 'If you can keep your head when those about you are losing theirs and blaming it on you', as Kipling wrote. If you can do that, then people will calm down and begin to think and work constructively.

In his Cabinet Room when he was Prime Minister, Harold Macmillan kept a card in front of him with this sentence in his own handwriting: 'Quiet, calm deliberation disentangles every knot'. That is a good practical rule of thumb for a leader to act upon.

Self-control, however, should not be confused with that peculiar Anglo-Saxon ailment known as the 'stiff upper lip'.

Calmness in Action

General Robert E. Lee was perhaps the finest military leader in the American Civil War. At the outset both sides sought him as their commander-in-chief but Lee's loyalty to his native state of Virginia drew him into the camp of the Confederacy. By skilful generalship and good leadership he waged a remarkably successful war against the North. But at the three-day battle of Gettysburg any hope of victory for the South suffered a severe setback. The decisive point came when an attack led by one of Lee's subordinates, General Pickett, failed. An eyewitness was present when news of this disaster reached Lee:

His face did not show the slightest disappointment, care or annoyance, and he addressed to every soldier he met a few words of encouragement. 'All will come right in the end, we'll talk it over afterwards.' And to a Brigade Commander speaking angrily of the heavy losses of his men: 'Never mind, General, all this has been my fault. It is I who have lost this fight, and you must help me out of it the best way you can.'

Leaders do not see themselves as unemotional or impersonal 'man-managers'. (Lord Slim once told me that the term 'man-management' was introduced to the Army because someone wanted to write a pamphlet to follow one entitled 'Mule Management!') Characteristically they do not think of people as 'human resources'. Indeed extending the principle that leaders should exemplify or personify the qualities expected or required in their working groups, it could be said that leaders should possess such natural human qualities as dignity and compassion. In a word, he should be humane.

Sometimes when we see the natural expression of that humanity we are astonished and delighted. For we expected to see a figurehead and we find a man. During the Second World War Hitler adamantly refused to go and see the bombed streets in Berlin, despite Goebbels pleading with him to do so for propaganda reasons. By contrast Churchill insisted on visiting the bombed areas of east London in 1940 and stood in the ruins of humble houses with tears streaming down his face. Lord Ismay, who was with him, tells how on that occasion a woman in the crowd which was surging around him said, 'Look, he's crying. He cares, he really cares!'; and in those few simple words that woman undoubtedly expressed the reaction that genuine humanity produces in all of us.

SUMMARY

The function of *controlling* involves both checking against standards and directing the course of work in progress. Supervising or overseeing implies that you as leader are watching the team at work, poised to intervene constructively if the need arises. That does not mean you should have no work of your own or never lend a hand. But primarily your responsibility for the whole team effort should come first. If you have performed the foregoing functions well and trained your team, it should become largely *self-controlling*. Meetings in particular call for skilled control by the chairman.

In organisations it is essential to set up *control systems*, which should be kept as simple as possible. Most industrial or commercial organisations that fail exhibit, among other things, poor financial controls. Therefore, controlling implies more than firmly being in charge. It requires skills with individuals, groups and organisations. It is useless to seek to control others if you cannot control yourself. 'In managing human affairs', said Lao-Tzu, 'there is no better rule than self-restraint.'

CHECKLIST: CONTROLLING

	Yes	No
Do you maintain a balance between controlling with too tight a rein and giving the group too much freedom to do as it pleases?	☐	☐
Are you able to co-ordinate work in progress, bringing all the several parts into a common, harmonious action in proper relation with each other?	☐	☐
On those occasions when you are directly involved with the 'technical' work, do you make arrangements so that the team requirements and the specific needs of its members are not ignored or overlooked?	☐	☐

What were the three characteristics of the most effective chairman of meetings you have come across?

1
2
3

When you are 'in the chair' do meetings run over the time allotted for them:

Never ☐   Sometimes ☐   Always ☐

| Does your department or unit have a proper budgeting system? | ☐ | ☐ |

Is the organisation you work for noted with customers on account of its control systems in the following areas:

Quality of product/service
Delivery
Keeping costs down
Safety

10 Evaluating

Appraising, evaluating, rating, assessing, judging and esti-
mating are all aspects of the basic function of valuing. These
ships can all sail here under the flagship of *evaluating*: the
ability to determine or fix the value of something. Like analysing and synthesising, the other two basic functions of intelligence, valuing enters into all of a leader's thinking and action.
The controlling function, for example, clearly involves some
evaluating of progress against yardsticks or standards. In this
section we shall concentrate on some specific skills which you
will need to acquire or develop as a leader, namely: assessing
consequences; evaluating team performance; appraising and
training individuals; judging people.

On judgement

Judgement is necessary because the Cabinet is the instrument
by which decisions are reached with a view to action, and
decisions stem from judgement. A Cabinet is not a place for
eloquence – one reason why good politicians are not always
good Cabinet Ministers. It is judgement which is needed to make
important decisions on imperfect knowledge in a limited time.
Men either have it, or they haven't. They can develop it, if they
have it; but cannot acquire it if they haven't.

Strength of character is required to stand up to criticism from
other Cabinet members, pressure from outside groups, and the
advice of civil servants.

It is also necessary when policies, on which the Cabinet has
agreed, are going through the doldrums, or are beginning to fail.
A man of character will neither be, nor seem to be, bowed down
by this. Nor will he be blown about by 'every wind of
vain doctrine'.

Clement Attlee

ASSESSING CONSEQUENCES

In all organisations there are some people who have a reputation for good judgement in the sense that they are adept at
assessing the consequences of any potential action inside and
outside the organisation. Equally we all know people who lack
judgement in this respect. In industry they are often responsible for triggering off strikes, stoppages or other breakdowns
in industrial relations.

In the decision-making or problem-solving process you will
have to assess the consequences of proposed courses of action
or solutions before making up your mind. It is helpful to bear
in mind that consequences can be divided into six categories,
which overlap considerably (see Fig. 10.1).

Probing the Consequences	
Type	Probing Questions
Desirable	What solid advantages has this course or solution in terms of the common purpose, aim or objective?
Undesirable	Has it unwelcome side-effects? Does it create more problems than it solves?
Manifest	What consequences – good or bad – are open to view now?
Latent	There will be consequences I cannot foresee now. Can I cut down their number by further thought or research? Have I sufficient resources to deal with possible contingencies?
Task	What are the technical consequences of adopting this method rather than that?
People	What will be the effects on (a) team (b) individuals (c) organisation (d) society (e) myself?

Fig. 10.1

In some instances you will be reduced to rough estimates or guesses about these consequences. But the greater the amount of science you bring to bear the more you can predict consequences with accuracy. Where possible turn estimates into calculations. In industry that means carrying out a rigorous profit/cost evaluation of the courses open.

With regard to 'people' consequences, a matter of vital concern to the leader, a common mistake is to guess instead of finding out by going and asking the people concerned. 'They will never agree to working extra shifts, that's for sure. They never have done in the past', said a board director. But that is an unexamined assumption. (Remember the dots and the matchsticks exercises!) Test that consequence to see if it is a real one – you may get a pleasant surprise.

Tony Hill, Chairman of Unilever UK Holdings Ltd., tells the following story from his experience.

We have all known for a long time that a group of people will work best together on a project if they all know and understand what are the facts, what is the objective and how it is proposed to achieve that objective.

I would like to give you a small example of how better understanding through better information can lead to better decisions. In 1960, when I was a director of a Unilever subsidiary in Germany, there were fears that West Berlin might be isolated and these circumstances produced a fair amount of panic buying particularly of such commodities as the washing products which we produced. The possibility of jacking up production quickly by instituting an extra shift for a period of some two weeks was discussed with the works council. The board met their leaders and explained the situation. After serious consideration *they* suggested to *us*: 'You will need special working for four weeks' (not the two management had suggested). 'If then the situation seems to be righting itself, with the longest notice you can give us we will go back to normal working.' This was the right decision and we knew it, we had not dared to ask for it because we thought they would refuse. But this kind of incident illustrates how the whole company was able to benefit from the fact that the elected representatives of the employees had been regularly kept informed with honest, factual information and, as a result, were able to make a valuable contribution to company plans.

Someone once summed up the decision-making process as (1) making the decision (2) implementing it, and (3) living with the consequences! You can develop your ability to assess those consequences in advance – except for the latent ones – by carefully analysing cause-and-effect in what happens. Gradually you identify patterns or tendencies. It becomes easier to predict what will happen. Your depth mind, the subconscious centre of your 10,000 million brain cells, can sometimes act as a computer in this respect, printing out warnings, judgements or expectations. An informed or educated depth mind, fed upon experience analysed and digested, is a valuable asset for any leader.

A Leader's Private Computer

Wrote the late Lord Thomson of Fleet: 'If I have any advice to pass on, it is this: If one wants to be successful, one must think until it hurts. One must worry a problem in one's mind until it seems there cannot be another aspect of it that hasn't been considered. Believe me, that is hard work and, from my close observation, I can say that there are few people indeed who are prepared to perform this arduous and tiring work.

But let me go further and assure you of this: while, in the early stages, it is hard work and one must accept it as such, later one will find that it is not so difficult, the thinking apparatus has become trained; it is trained even to do some of the thinking subconsciously. The pressure that one had to use on one's poor brain in the early stages no longer is necessary; the hard grind is rarely needed; one's mental computer arrives at decisions instantly or during a period when the brain seems to be resting. It is only the rare and most complex problems that require the hard toil of protracted mental effort.'

After I was Sixty (Hamish Hamilton)

EVALUATING TEAM PERFORMANCE

In working enterprises it is often valuable to have a 'de-briefing' session after a particular project. This gives you the chance to evaluate the performance of the group as a whole in relation to the task. First you should have a realistic and honest statement of results in terms of the following:

Success	Objectives all achieved
Limited success	Some objectives or part of the objective attained but not others
Failure	None of the objectives achieved

Then you should move on to the evaluation proper. You can either initiate this phase by giving your own views, or invite comments from the group as a whole. Unless you are a very experienced leader, it is best always to follow the simple drill of identifying the good points first – what went well – and then coming onto the points for improvement. These should include constructive ways in which the team performance as a whole can be changed for the better. You may take decisions on the spot to effect these changes or choose to think about it for a day or two. Group meetings for 'de-briefing' purposes are usually not the right place to deal with individual failings unless you want to make an example of someone for the benefit of the group as a whole.

At de-briefing meetings, however, you can tackle any particular problems that have caused the group to fragment into independent rather than inter-dependent parts. The film *Twelve o'Clock High* provides a good illustration of the latter. During one de-briefing meeting, while the 918 Bomb Group is still sustaining heavy losses over enemy territory, Savage finds that some individuals are putting their buddies first.

Savage:	Pettigill!
Pettigill:	Yes, Sir.
Savage:	We were plenty lucky to have only one loss on this strike. Why did you break formation?'
Pettigill:	Well, Sir, Ackermann was in trouble, two engines on fire, and we were getting enemy fighters. I figured I'd better stay back with him and try to cover him going into the target. But he couldn't make it.
Savage:	(after a pause): Ackermann a pretty good friend of yours?
Pettigill:	My room-mate, Sir.
Savage:	So for the sake of your room-mate, you violated Group integrity. Every gun on a B.17 is designed to give the Group maximum defensive fire-power, that's what I mean by Group integrity. When you pull a B.17 out of a formation you reduce the defensive power of the Group by ten guns. A crippled aeroplane has to be expendable. The one thing which is never expendable is your obligation to this Group. This Group,

	this Group, that has to be your loyalty, your only reason for being! Stovall!
Stovall:	Yes, Sir.
Savage:	Have the Billeting Officer work out a complete reassignment of quarters so that every man has a new room-mate.
Stovall:	Very well, Sir.

In this scene Savage shows considerable *skill*, which is worth exploring further. He *senses* a problem and asks a *probing question* to complete his diagnosis: 'Is Ackermann a pretty good friend of yours?' He *orders* the re-allocation of rooms to deal with what he has diagnosed as a *general problem*, and he *reiterates the group standard* he is trying to set: in this case putting the group first and self second.

APPRAISING AND TRAINING INDIVIDUALS

The appraisal interview is a familiar term in the management jargon. This is a regular interview, sometimes as little as once a year, when a manager sits down with his subordinate and appraises the work of the subordinate against his objectives. 'Don't tell me that the man is doing good work', said Andrew Carnegie to one of his plant bosses. 'Tell me what good work he is doing'.

During an appraisal interview you should create an environment where you can have a constructive dialogue with a subordinate (or superior or colleague for that matter) on the following agenda:

1 past performance
2 future work to be done, targets, priorities, standards and strategies
3 matching perceptions of what they can reasonably expect of each other in order to achieve a sound working relationship
4 improving skill, knowledge, behaviour

Fig. 10.2, based upon an article by Lawrence Russell of the Engineering Industry Training Board[1], sets out some useful guidelines for appraiser and appraised.

| Performance Appraisal Interviewing ||
Guidelines	Notes
1 Ensure the necessary data is available	To substantiate discussion and to keep it factual, all documents, reports, data or back-up information should be readily available for the interview
2 Put the other person at ease	Both parties should try to be relaxed, open minded, aware of the purpose of the meeting, committed to its purpose and be prepared to discuss things calmly and frankly. If there is undue tension or distrust much of the value of the interview will be lost
3 Control pace and direction of interview	Both parties have a part to play to control and influence the pace and direction of the interview to keep it relevant, helpful and work-orientated.
4 Listen . . . listen . . . listen	The most difficult part of the interview is for both parties to really listen to each other. Listening is more than not speaking, it is emptying the mind of preconceived ideas or prejudices. It is being willing to consider another person's point of view and if that view is better than the one previously held, being humble enough – and big enough – to accept it.
5 Don't be destructively critical	Where possible, people should be encouraged to be self-critical – critical of their own performance and motivated to improve. This approach goes a long way to remove the unnecessary conflict from the meeting.
6 Review performance systematically	It is important to stick to the facts – facts which can be substantiated – and that's where the relevant back-up information comes in handy.

Fig. 10.2

Performance Appraisal Interviewing	
Guidelines	Notes
7 Discuss future action	This is an opportunity to discuss with one another – almost on equal terms – what has been done, how it can best be done, who will do it, when and to what standard. Any suggestions put forward or agreements reached should be written down while they are still fresh in each others mind. This becomes an action plan.
8 Be prepared to discuss potential or aspirations	The question of the individual's potential for future promotion doesn't always arise, but it is wise to be prepared for it. A person who is considered by his boss not to be ready for promotion may feel he has the right to know the reason why not, and many expect suggestions which might improve his or her potential.
9 Identify essential training/ development required	The final part of the interview is usually devoted to discussing the training and counselling which may be required in order to carry out the agreed action plan. This should also be written down – what essential training or development is needed, will it be given on-the-job or elsewhere, who will give it and when?
10 Avoid obvious pitfalls	Such things as: • talking too much and hogging the conversation • introducing unnecessary conflict • jumping to hasty conclusions • unjustly blaming others – particularly those who are not present to defend themselves • expecting the impossible – like wanting a person to change significant character traits overnight • and lastly, making promises which neither party may be able to keep

Fig. 10.2 (continued)

At the end of the interview or shortly afterwards, any agreed future actions should be written down. What has to be done? When? To what standard? Here is a simple example of how such a programme can be recorded:

PERSONAL ACTION PLAN – Resulting from appraisal interview dated			
Action or targets agreed	To be taken by	Standard to be achieved	Date start/ finish

Do not expect too much from a system of formal performance appraisal interviews. Certainly if they are not followed up by action from both the appraiser and the appraisee they can soon degenerate into empty rituals. But the results of a good appraisal, when linked with good counselling, include

---

On-the-job training

General Horrocks recalled one incident which revealed Montgomery's ability to develop the individual, even at the higher levels of leadership.

On the day after the battle [Alam Halfa] I was sitting in my headquarters purring with satisfaction. The battle had been won and I had not been mauled in the process. What could be better? Then in came a liaison officer from 8th Army headquarters bringing me a letter in Monty's even hand. This is what he said:
'Dear Horrocks,
Well done – but you must remember that you are now a corps commander and not a divisional commander . . .'
He went on to list four or five things which I had done wrong, mainly because I had interfered too much with the tasks of my subordinate commanders. The purring stopped abruptly.
Perhaps I wasn't quite such a heaven-sent general after all. But the more I thought over the battle, the more I realised that Monty was right. So I rang him up and said, 'Thank you very much.'
I mention this because Montgomery was one of the few commanders who tried to train the people who worked under him. Who else, on the day after his first major victory, which had altered the whole complexion of the war in the Middle East, would have taken the trouble to write a letter like this in his own hand to one of his subordinate commanders?

Lieut. General Sir Brian Horrocks
A Full Life, Collins, 1956

better team-work, improved commitment and the development of knowledge, skill and character.

Therefore, you should see the formal system as at best a
safety net for a process that should be going on continually.
As the leader you should be continually assessing the value of
each individual's contribution and giving him feedback on
how he is doing. Sometimes individuals, especially the over-
modest ones, may genuinely undervalue some action or function they perform. It is a kind of occupational inferiority
complex. The leader can correct this misjudgement. He may
also, as we have seen, have occasion to point out the short-
falls in objectives.

A leader, however, is not in the seat of a judge in the
lawcourt impartially appraising someone's actions while they
stand in the dock. He is out to improve performance. Therefore he has to be skilled in communicating both his perceptions of the strengths and the weaknesses of the individual
concerned. He must have data or information at hand to back
up any observation he gives. Above all, he must put his
suggestions across so that they are acceptable and actionable
by the individual. The best way to do that is to ask the
individual to appraise his own performance against standing
or continuing aims and specific objectives. Then to agree with
him an action plan for the future.

Thus, the function of appraising an individual's performance is only useful if it is the prelude to some form of learning
or training. Even if the result of the interview is that you
dismiss that person, or transfer him to another group, it can
still be presented in a positive light as a lesson you have
learned together. As a leader you need to be in part a teacher
or trainer of people. Conversely, a teacher has to be something
of a leader.

Is it possible to teach yourself specific techniques, such as
asking questions of different kinds which may be useful in
appraisal interviews? The following could be useful examples.

Opening	'Tell me about your sales programme'
Probing	'Is that the first time you failed to meet a target?'
Factual	'Where were you when it happened?'
Reflective	'You obviously feel very disappointed and upset at what was said to you'

Leading	'I suppose you will improve that next year?'
Limited choice	'If you had to choose between general personnel work and industrial relations, which would it be?'

What matters more, however, is to take seriously your responsibilities for *developing the individual* as his mentor throughout the year, not just for an hour or two in a formal or semi-formal interview. You should be able to offer him your practical wisdom. Someone once defined wisdom as a combination of three elements: *experience, intelligence and goodness*. Unfortunately unless your subordinate appraises *you* highly in all three respects, he is unlikely to want to learn from you. As Winston Churchill once said, 'I cannot stand being taught – but I enjoy learning'. What is it in you that makes people want to learn from you? Granted you have a modicum of wisdom, it is best to see yourself not as a coach training a sportsman, but as a more experienced artist sitting down beside another and commenting helpfully on the work in hand. Remember Cicero's definition of an orator: 'a good man skilled in speaking'. The development of a subordinate may well test your goodness as well as your skill as a teacher. But it is one of those activities that can make leadership such a rewarding experience.

JUDGING PEOPLE

You may hear it said about some leaders who are outstanding in other respects: 'He is no judge of character. Some of the appointments he has made have been disastrous'.

Conversely some people – not all leaders – have a natural flair for forming accurate judgements about people and how they are likely to behave in certain situations. If you have some natural ability as a judge you can develop it by observation, experience and study. It is especially instructive to check appointments made by others in your organisation against your own knowledge of that person on the one hand and the requirements of the job on the other. Would you have made that appointment? Did it turn out to be a good, average or weak decision in terms of results?

Oliver Cromwell at work

Cromwell proved to be an excellent judge of men. The appointments he made in the New Model Army were based upon merit and spirit. He showed this gift early on in selected men for his troop of horse and later for his regiment. In 1645, while still a colonel, aged 46 years, he served under General Sir William Waller in the West, who left this memoir of him.

'And here I cannot but mention the wonder which I have oft times had to see this eagle in his eirey. He at this time had never shown extraordinary parts, nor do I think that he did himself believe that he had them, for although he was blunt he did not bear himself with pride or disdain. As an officer he was obedient, and did never dispute my orders nor argue upon them. He did, indeed, seem to have great cunning, and while he was cautious of his own words, not putting forth too many lest they should betray his thoughts, he made others talk until he had as it were sifted them and known their inmost designs. A noticeable instance was his discovering in one short conversation with one Captain Giles (a great favourite with the Lord General and whom he most confided in) that although his words were full of zeal and his actions seemingly brave, his heart was not with the cause. And in fine, this man did shortly after join the enemy at Oxford with 23 stout fellows.'

The practice of having favourites is a dangerous one for leaders on several scores. First, it breaks up team unity. Research has shown that, if an Arctic traveller makes a favourite of one husky among his sledge dogs, the effectiveness of the whole team sharply deteriorates. Secondly, the favourite is an expression of your judgement about people. If others, who know their colleagues better than you do, fail to agree upon your apparently high estimate of his worth, then your credibility suffers. Thirdly, favourites advance by astutely recognising the social and esteem needs of their bosses. If they sense that you like flattery, they will lay it on with a trowel. Some people are natural courtiers and will vie for your favour with such gifts. In time your judgement can become impaired and forget the trivial reasons why you have patronised them and you may actually promote them into responsible positions, where they surely fail.

Assuming that you have remained impartial and evenhanded (although it is only human to like some people more than others), the best way to improve your judgements and decisions about people is to take them slowly and work harder at them. There should be times when you actively work on the question by analysing your impressions and discussing them with others, followed by times when you relegate the matter to your subconscious or depth mind for further resolution.

People decisions

Among the effective executives I have had occasion to observe, there have been people who make decisions fast, and people who make them rather slowly. But without exception, they make personnel decisions slowly and they make them several times before they really commit themselves.

Alfred P. Sloan, Jr., former head of General Motors, the world's largest manufacturing company, was reported never to make a personnel decision the first time it came up. He made a tentative judgement, and even that took several hours as a rule. Then, a few days or weeks later, he tackled the question again, as if he had never worked on it before. Only when he came up with the same name two or three times in a row was he willing to go ahead. Sloan had a deserved reputation for the 'winners' he picked. But when asked about his secret, he is reported to have said: 'No secret – I have simply accepted that the first name I come up with is likely to be the wrong name - and I therefore retrace the whole process of thought and analysis a few times before I act.' Yet Sloan was far from a patient man.

Few executives make personnel decisions of such impact. But all effective executives I have had occasion to observe have learned that they have to give several hours of continuous and uninterrupted thought to decisions on people if they hope to come up with the right answer.

Peter Drucker,
The Effective Executive, Heinemann, 1967

SELF-EVALUATION

Like the other functions you can apply the principle of evaluating to yourself and your work. Indeed, one major objective for you is to form a clear vision of what *quality* in leadership means. Then you can appraise your progress in the light of it at regular intervals. For the best way to learn leadership is to do your present job as well as possible and to carefully monitor your own performance. If you can develop the insight to monitor your leadership performance, then even mistakes and failures will disclose positive lessons.

SUMMARY

The ability to *evaluate* is an important leadership function. In this chapter it has been discussed under four headings: assessing consequences, evaluating team performance, appraising and training individuals and judging people. A crucial element in decision making is evaluating the alternatives in terms of their consequences – technical, financial and human. Unless you can evaluate team performance with skill, the people working for you will miss a vital part of the feedback which should be coming their way. Appraising the contribution of individuals is a continuing activity, part of the process of calling forth the best from people. The higher you have risen as a leader the more important it is for you to develop good judgement about people. Avoid having favourites. The test of your ability in this respect lies in the performance of the people you have appointed. 'By their fruits you shall know them'.

CHECKLIST: EVALUATING

In assessing the outcome of possible courses of action or solutions do you take time to consider the consequences for the team and the individual as well as the task?

Always ☐   Sometimes ☐   Rarely ☐

How do you rate yourself as far as judgement in decision-making is concerned?

Good   Your decisions usually have the predicted   ....
              results; you can foresee consequences and
              are rarely surprised at outcomes. Shrewd
              and discerning at all times.

Average   Your predictions of consequences are   ....
              accurate about half the time. Your
              commonsense is often proved right.

Weak   Poor judgement often mars your   ....
              performance. You tend to guess too much
              what will result from a given decision, and
              are frequently wrong.

How would you assess yourself as an appraiser of the work of an individual?

Good   You hold regular appraisal meetings and   ....
              do quite a lot on a day-to-day basis. You
              always support general points with
              evidence. You tend always to praise first
              and criticise second. Your appraising
              usually results in better work performance.

Average	Sometimes it seems to work, other times .... not. You find it difficult to hit the right note with some people. Quite frankly, awkward people, who don't want to learn, defeat you.
Weak	You lose credibility every time you try to .... appraise someone. It usually ends up in an argument. You tell them, but they refuse to listen.

What is your record in judging people? In selecting and promoting individuals, which of the following statements characterises your approach?

You can always pick a winner, and never consult   ....
anyone else or seek specialist advice

You go by first impressions. Even if you think you are   ....
wrong you usually return to them in the end

You take people decisions slowly. You like to consult   ....
others who know the person, often on a confidential
basis. You do not trust your own first thought

You like to see a person in a variety of different   ....
situations before making up your mind. Track record
is an important factor to you, more so than
psychological tests and the like

You rarely choose a person on technical grounds alone, ...
unless he is working on his own. You try to see him in
the context of being a team leader or member, and
judge if he will get on well with the individuals in that
group

Would you regard your regular evaluation of your own performance as
(a) more rigorous (b) less searching or (c) about the same as your
evaluation of others?

(a) ☐   (b) ☐   (c) ☐

11 Motivating

As a leader you have to be able to get the group and its individual members moving – or keep them moving – in the desired direction. This general ability to move and excite people to action is now called *motivation*. The subjects of your motivating activity will be the *team* and the *individual*. By extension it will come to include the *organisation* as well.

In the general theory upon which this book is based you will not have to motivate people at work in the sense of supplying them with a motive. Both group and individual are already self-motivating. The group and organisation are moved to achieve the task needs and to maintain themselves as social unities with a distinct identity. These are interactive. The individual (see again p. 119) has needs common to us all which are met to varying degrees by taking part in work with others. The common task provides opportunities for developing a sense of achievement, gaining status and recognition, while the group opens the door to social needs being met. Money is primarily a means of exchange, which allows us to convert work in one specialised activity (such as nursing or building roads) directly into the results of other kinds of work – food, drink, shelter and warmth – the means for meeting our physiological needs.

This kind of perspective on people, based largely on the contributions of such psychologists as Maslow, began to influence industry and management in the late 1950s. Douglas McGregor pointed out that managers often operated mainly under one of two sets of contrasting explicit or implicit assumptions about people, which he labelled theory X and theory Y,[1] see Fig. 11.1.

Assumptions about Man	
Theory X	Theory Y
Man dislikes work and will avoid it if he can.	Work is necessary to man's psychological growth. Man wants to be interested in his work and, under the right conditions, he can enjoy it.
Man must be forced or bribed to put out the right effort.	Man will direct himself towards an accepted target.
Man would rather be directed than accept responsibility, which he avoids.	Man will seek, and accept responsibility under the right conditions. The discipline a man imposes on himself is more effective, and can be more severe, than any imposed on him.
Man is motivated mainly by money. Man is motivated by anxiety about his security.	Under the right conditions man is motivated by the desire to realise his own potential.
Most men have little creativity – except when it comes to getting round management rules!	Creativity and ingenuity are widely distributed and grossly underused.

Fig. 11.1

McGregor made the point that what we believe about a person can help that person to behave in that way (*the self-fulfilling prophecy*). If you tell someone you believe that they are bone idle, for example, they will tend to live up to your prediction. If you have a high regard for them, although that is not strictly justified by the facts, they may well rise to meet your expectations.

Natural leaders have always acted on that assumption. They hold a creative or strategic belief in people, despite evidence to the contrary. 'Trust men and they will be true to you', said Emerson. 'Treat them greatly and they will show themselves great.'

The Pygmalion Effect

In George Bernard Shaw's *Pygmalion*, Eliza Doolittle explains:

"You see, really and truly, apart from the things anyone can pick up (the dressing and the proper way of speaking and so on), the difference between a lady and a flower girl is not how she behaves, but how she's treated. I shall always be a flower girl to Professor Higgins, because he always treats me as a flower girl, and always will, but I know I can be a lady to you, because you always treat me as a lady, and always will."

Pygmalion was a sculptor in Greek mythology who carved a statue of a beautiful woman that subsequently was brought to life. George Bernard Shaw's play, *Pygmalion* (the basis for the musical hit, "My Fair Lady"), has a somewhat similar theme; the essence is that one person, by his effort and will, can transform another person. And in the world of management many executives play Pygmalion-like roles in developing able subordinates and in stimulating their performance. What is the secret of their success? How are they different from managers who fail to develop top-notch subordinates?[2]

Another expression of this understanding of man as essentially self-motivating appeared in the work of Frederick Herzberg, another American Professor of Psychology, who involved himself far more than Maslow in industry. In the mid-1950s Herzberg and his associates interviewed 203 engineers and accountants in Pittsburg to find out why they found some events in their working lives highly satisfying and others highly dissatisfying. Herzberg divided the factors involved into two factors, which he called 'motivators' and 'hygiene factors'. The motivators provided longer-lasting satisfaction to individuals. The hygiene factors cause us dissatisfaction if they are wrong. But if you give a person more of a hygiene factor you will only either reduce their dissatisfaction or else give them a short lived sense of satisfaction.[3]

Herzberg's 'two-factor' theory (see Fig. 11.2) has been the cause of much controversial debate. Like most black-and-white, 'either-or' pieces of analysis, binary interpretation achieves the appearance of simplicity but only at the cost of sacrificing elements of the more complex truth. Money, for example, cannot be regarded as a hygiene factor: it can serve as a tangible and necessary expression of recognition in some spheres. Nonetheless, Herzberg has had a powerful influence on the movement to increase job satisfaction in industry, a practical application of the wider understanding of individual needs.

Herzberg's Two-factor Theory	
What motivates or satisfies people at work is not the opposite to what demotivates or dissatisfies them. There are two separate sets of factors at work. This list describes those identified by Herzberg as motivators.	
Factor	Definition
Achievement	Sense of bringing something to a successful conclusion, completing a job, solving a problem, making a successful sale. The sense of achievement is in proportion to the size of the challenge
Recognition	Acknowledgement of a person's contribution; appreciation of work by company or colleagues; rewards for merit
Job interest	Intrinsic appeal of job; variety rather than repetition; holds interest and is not monotonous or boring
Responsibility	Being allowed to use discretion at work; shown trust by company; having authority to make decisions; accountable for the work of others
Advancement	Promotion in status or job, or the prospect of it.

Fig. 11.2

Although Herzberg includes 'supervision' in his set of hygiene factors – those which cause great dissatisfaction when they are not met or are 'wrong' – he is clearly mistaken on this point. Leadership, a word he did not use, is more than just part of someone's job context: in many instances it is integral to the job itself. You only have to look at the list above to see that leaders can play a large part in the 'motivators'. Here are some of the ways described in this book.

ACHIEVEMENT

The function of evaluating means that the leader will give both the group and the individual feedback when the task is achieved. Sometimes there is direct feedback to the group or individual not involving the leader, as when a football team scores the winning goal in a cup final or a construction crew contemplate a finished suspension bridge. In other situations the feedback may come via the leader, who then needs to communicate success to the group.

> The training department at Aerospace Simulators Ltd. had worked very hard to lay on a new series of courses for supervisors in leadership training. The girls in the office had worked sometimes through their lunch hours to finish the paper work. After the first course the line manager running it made a special point of going into the training department and giving information to the typists about its success, otherwise they might never have heard about the end-product of all that work. 'Well, it was certainly worth the extra work to hear that it is going to make that sort of contribution to the company', said one of the secretaries afterwards.

RECOGNITION

Managers are sometimes tempted to claim the credit for themselves after a success. If so, they are thinking of their own advancement. As a leader, however, you should seize every opportunity to motivate people by recognising their worth, services or contribution. Credit has to be shared, while you take the blame for yourself. At the first level of leadership, good leaders naturally meet recognition needs by acknowledging the contributions of individuals or of their team as a whole. If they receive some symbolic reward, such as a medal or citation, they interpret it as a recognition of the group's achievements as a whole. Equally, at a higher level, the leader may show recognition of the contributions of groups, departments or units to the success or prospects of success of the whole organisation.

The individuals or groups with high prestige or obviously vital functions tend to get all the recognition. A wise and able leader, however, will make sure that the apparently weak and insignificant individuals or groups also get their fair share of recognition. This equalising work both promotes or builds up a sense of being a team and also meets the needs of some individuals (or groups) who would otherwise receive no recognition in the world's market place, where such rewards go naturally to the most powerful, best-looking, most active or simply the most apt at edging themselves into the limelight.

After Henry Saunders, the new Chairman of Aerospace Simulators had been with the company for a month he embarked on a series of visits to talk directly to the staff at the six factories in the United Kingdom, France and Holland. 'What is behind that door?', he asked divisional head office. 'Oh, just the telephone exchange', replied the manager in charge. 'Lunch is ready now, Chairman . . .' But Mr. Saunders had already walked into the exchange. He congratulated the supervisor and operators on the excellent job they were doing for the company and emphasised the need for swift, courteous and economical communications if the company was going to achieve its objectives in the coming year.

The Forgotten Army

The Fourteenth Army in India and Burma during the Second World War thought of itself as the 'Forgotten Army' before Field Marshal Slim took command. Within it certain units and individuals felt even more forgotten than the rest. By energetic leadership Slim set about changing this situation.

'The fighting soldier facing the enemy can see that what he does, whether he is brave or craven, matters to his comrades and directly influences the result of the battle. It is harder for the man working on the road far behind, the clerk checking stores in a dump, the headquarter's telephone operator monotonously plugging through his calls, the sweeper carrying out his menial tasks, the quartermaster's orderly issuing bootlaces in a reinforcement camp – it is hard for these and a thousand others to see that they too matter. Yet every one of the half-million in the army – and it was many more later – had to be made to see where his task fitted into the whole, to realise what depended on it, and to feel pride and satisfaction in doing it well.

We, my commanders and I, talked to units, to collections of officers, to headquarters, to little groups of men, to individual soldiers casually met as we moved around. I learnt, too, that one did not need to be an orator to be effective. Two things were necessary: first to know what you were talking about, and second and most important, to believe it yourself. I found that if one kept the bulk of one's talk to the material things that men were interested in, food, pay, leave, beer, mails, and the progress of operations, it was safe to end on a higher note – the spiritual foundations (belief in the cause) – and I always did.

To convince the men in the less spectacular or less obviously important jobs that they were very much part of the army, my commanders and I made it our business to visit these units, to show an interest in them, and to tell them how we and the rest of the army depended upon them. There are in the army, and for that matter any big organisation, very large numbers of people whose existence is only remembered when something for which they are responsible goes wrong. Who thinks of the telephone operator until he fails to get his connection, of the cipher officer until he makes a mistake in his decoding, of the orderlies who carry papers about a big headquarters until they take them to the wrong people, of the cook until he makes a particularly foul mess of the interminable bully? Yet they are important. It was harder to get this over to the Indian subordinates. They were often drawn from the lower castes, quite illiterate, and used to being looked down upon by their higher-caste fellow-townsmen or villagers. With them, I found I had great success by using the simile of a clock. 'A clock is like an army', I used to tell them. 'There's a main spring, that's the Army Commander, who makes it all go; then there are other springs, driving the wheels round, those are his generals. The wheels are the officers and men. Some are big wheels, very important, they are the chief staff officers and the colonel sahibs. Other wheels are little ones, that do not look at all important. They are like you. Yet stop one of those little wheels and see what happens to the rest of the clock! They are important!'

We played on this very human desire of every man to feel himself and his work important, until one of the most striking things about our army was the way the administrative, labour and non-combatant units acquired a morale which rivalled that of the fighting formations. They felt they shared directly in the triumphs of the Fourteenth Army and that its success and its honour were in their hands as much as anybody's. Another way in which we made every man feel he was part of the show was by keeping him, whatever his rank, as far as was practicable in the picture of what was going on around him. This, of course, was easy with staff officers and similar people by means of conferences held daily or weekly when each branch or department could explain what it had been doing and what it hoped to do. At these conferences they not only discussed things as a team, but what was equally important, actually saw themselves as a team. For the men, talks by their officers and visits to the information centres which were established in every unit took the place of those conferences.

Field Marshal Lord Slim,
Defeat into Victory, Cassell, 1956

JOB INTEREST

If work is to be restructured in order to allow more job satisfaction someone has to have the vision to undertake it and the consultative skills to bring about the change. That means leadership. In particular it calls upon the leader's organising ability, the subject of the next section.

RESPONSIBILITY

The leader is accountable for the results of his group. Marshal Pétain, when asked after the First World War, 'Marshal, did you personally win the Battle of Verdun?' replied, 'I've no idea, but I know very well who would have lost it'. But as a leader you should share the sense of responsibility as widely as possible.

The clue to developing responsibility is to extend the boundaries of trust. There can be an element of risk in this process, but there is no other practical alternative. As the Headmaster of Eton College once said to me, 'If you trust boys they will let you down – but if you do not trust them they will *do* you down.' Trust, however, can be expressed in many ways and in varying degrees. Delegation, the entrusting of authority to someone to act as your deputy, is a major expression of trust and a means of creating responsibility. But delegation has some inherent risks that make otherwise excellent leaders reluctant to do it.

At Aerospace Simulators Ltd. the new Chairman soon diagnosed a lack of proper delegation as a major problem. His predecessor, the entrepreneurial founder of the company, had kept authority and decision making firmly in his own hands. He even chose the size of paperclips. Cluttered up with so many minor decisions, he took a long time to make up his mind. Able people had become frustrated. Saunders delegated real authority to the three divisional heads. He pushed decision making down the line as far as it would go. He also delegated much of his secondary work to his staff, such as keeping his appointments diary. One divisional head and three factory managers proved not to be capable and had to go. Saunders believed in delegation – not abrogation. He checked up at regular intervals to see if all was well. He insisted on people coming back to him if they had a problem they could not solve. 'The work is often done differently than I would have done it', he admits, 'but I can now get on with my primary job of leading the company as a whole'.

ADVANCEMENT

Leaders play a vital part in promoting people. That gives them a certain power to motivate ambitious and able subordinates. They may not have the necessary jobs in their gift directly, but their word is often influential if not decisive. You can often motivate such an individual by reminding him that the prospects for advancement in positions or status do exist.

Of course promotion is not a motivating force if it is not related to merit and performance. No one is going to work harder if advancement is reserved for the company's 'blue-eyed boys'. By stressing that ability and results are the necessary condition for promotion, you can create the right bracing atmosphere to motivate people to give their best.

Stephen Nichols, the marketing manager of the second largest division in Aerospace Simulators, was young, energetic and able. His performance record was also outstanding. The Chairman, who had been studying the files of key personnel, invited him to come in and discuss his prospects. 'Quite honestly, Mr. Saunders, I have been looking elsewhere for a job', said Nichols. 'Well, you can stop looking', said Saunders with a smile. 'I should like you to take over running our largest factory at Birmingham. Are you interested? If you can make a success of it you will be in line for appointment as a divisional chief executive within the next five years'. Nichols took the job.

Therefore, if you examine closely all the factors which positively motivate people at work, you can see that good leadership plays an important part in all of them. Consider your reactions to Herzberg's Hygiene Factors (see Fig. 11.3) those elements that have the power to dissatisfy you if they are inadequate, but do not provide more than modest or short-term satisfactions?

Hygiene Factors	
Company policy and administration	Availability of clearly defined policies; degree of 'red tape', adequacy of communication; efficiency of organisation
Supervision	Accessibility, competence and personality of the boss
Interpersonal relations	The relations with supervisors, subordinates and colleagues; the quality of social life at work
Salary	The total rewards package, such as salary, pension, company car and other 'perks'
Status	A person's position or rank in relation to others, symbolised by title, parking space, car, size of offices, furnishings
Job security	Freedom from insecurity, such as loss of position or loss of employment altogether
Personal life	The effect of a person's work on family life e.g. stress, unsocial hours or moving house
Working conditions	The physical environment in which work is done; the degree of discomfort it causes

Fig. 11.3

Leadership enters into all these factors whether we wish it to or not. If poor organisation and an apparently unfair rewards system leaves people dissatisfied, someone has to organise things properly, and that 'someone' is usually a leader. The following section explores that organising function more fully. Good leadership resolves most of the dissatisfying factors implicit in being supervised and working with others: much of this book has been concerned with just those interpersonal relations.

Your leadership should also contribute to reducing insecurity. Once I worked as a deckhand in an Arctic trawler. The captain rarely came down from the bridge. He had delegated the leadership of the deckhands to the first mate. But just seeing him up there beside the helm in those winter storms off Iceland gave me a feeling of security. If you know you have the right leader at the wheel, as Britain felt in 1940 when Winston Churchill became Prime Minister, it generates a feeling of security even in the worst hour of corporate stress.

Status as one's position or rank in relation to others is an inescapable fact of life in working groups and organisations. Roughly speaking, higher status goes to those individuals who contribute more or hold the more responsible jobs. Most dissatisfaction over status is caused by apparently petty grievances over status symbols, such as parking space, offices or job titles. These often are symptoms of a deeper disease. For example, a very competitive person may make an issue of not having an office of his own because he sees that a potential rival has one, and he fears that he is being left behind in the race for promotion. Here the cause – insecurity – must be treated, not the symptom.

Personal problems may be caused by the effect of work on family life or the reverse process – some unhappiness at home which is causing difficulties at work. A good leader is sensitive to the individual: he can detect changes in norms of behaviour. As a leader it is important for you to demonstrate in

---

The Stallman's Tale

While writing this book I happened to drive down to the fruit and vegetable market in Guildford one Saturday morning to meet my wife who was doing the shopping. As I waited for her I saw an old age pensioner sieving potatoes behind one of the canvas stalls. He noticed our children through the open hatch-door of the car and came over to talk to them. He told me he had lost his two children in the Blitz. And two brothers, too. 'Do you know, I was Chief Petty Officer to Admiral Mountbatten in Malta during the war. The morning I heard that my brother was missing on a bombing raid over Germany he came into the office. "Why are you looking so down, Chief," he said. I told him, "Because I think my brother is dead". You know what he did? He went away and telegraphed to the Air Ministry in London and got them to find out about my brother. When they let him know what had happened some days later he came in and told me. He was an officer and a gentleman, he was.' Forty years had passed, but that act of leadership still lived in his mind.

some way or other that you are aware and that you do care. Even if you can do little or nothing, as in the case of a bereavement, the very fact of showing your sympathy does matter. In many instances, however, you can do something yourself to remove the obstacle which is damming and diverting his natural motivation.

SUMMARY

Human motives have their sources in the deeper needs and values within people. A need that becomes conscious is called a want. A leader can sometimes help the process by which needs are transformed into wants. He can also work with each individual to realise those wants in the context of the common task and the common life of group or organisation. Thus you have to keep the three-circles diagram in mind all the time in the early stages of your career as a leader. For motivation is not to be limited to the individual needs circle. It springs from hidden sources in the task and team circles as well. The circles overlap in theory; in practice it is your responsibility as leader to manage that overlap, to ensure that it happens in the most fruitful way. That means checking that the physiological and security needs of the individual are met. Beyond those come the 'higher' needs. If motivation and job satisfaction are to be good, not just adequate or weak, each individual must:

1 feel a sense of personal achievement in the job he is doing, that he is making a worthwhile contribution to the objectives of the group or section
2 feel that the job itself is challenging, is demanding the best of him, is giving him the responsibility to match his capabilities
3 receive adequate recognition for his achievements
4 have control over those aspects of his job which have been delegated to him
5 feel that he, as an individual, is developing, that he is advancing in experience and ability

To provide the right climate and opportunities for these needs to be met for each individual in the group is possibly the most difficult and certainly the most challenging and rewarding of the leader's tasks. 'The test of leadership', said John Buchan, 'is not to put greatness into humanity but to elicit it, for the greatness is there already'.

CHECKLIST: MOTIVATING

	Yes	No
Have you agreed with each of your subordinates his main targets and continuing responsibilities, together with standards of performance, so that you can both recognise achievement?	☐	☐
Do you recognise the contribution of each member of the group and encourage other team members to do the same?	☐	☐
In the event of success, do you acknowledge it and build on it? In the event of setbacks, do you identify what went well and give constructive guidance for improving future performance?	☐	☐
Can you delegate more? Can you give more discretion over decisions and more accountability to a sub-group or individual?	☐	☐
Do you show to those that work with you that you trust them, or do you hedge them around with unnecessary controls?	☐	☐
Are there adequate opportunities for training and (where necessary) re-training?	☐	☐
Do you encourage each individual to develop his capacities to the full?	☐	☐
Is the overall performance of each individual regularly reviewed in face-to-face discussion?	☐	☐
Does financial reward match contribution?	☐	☐
Do you make sufficient time to talk and listen, so that you understand the unique (and changing) profile of needs and wants in each person, so that you can work with the grain of nature rather than against it?	☐	☐
Do you encourage able people with the prospect of promotion within the organisation, or – if that is impossible – counsel them to look elsewhere for the next position fitting their merit?	☐	☐

Can you think of a manager by name who (a) delegates more effectively (b) less effectively than you do? What are the results in each case?

(a)

(b)

12 Organising

Organising is the function of arranging or forming into a coherent unity or functional whole. It can mean systematic planning as well, but that is a function we have already covered. Here organising means more the structuring that has to be done if people are to work as a unit with each element performing its proper part. As Alfred Sloan, the President of General Motors, observed, it is essentially concerned with getting right the relations of the whole and the parts. It is a manifestation of perhaps a deep vocational impulse to impose or bring order in place of chaos. Order is the value that lies behind society, just as freedom is the value that lies behind the individual. A balance needs to be struck in any group or organisation between order and freedom.

Just as there are leaders who prove to be extremely weak as organisers, especially when they are promoted beyond the primary group level higher up the organisation, so there are some who have a genius for organising but lack potential or developed ability in the other major functions. Assuming that you already have the raw materials of organising ability and some experience in organisations, the objective of this section is to sharpen your skills as an organiser.

ORGANISING THE GROUP

In order to achieve anything you may have to give your group some structure, especially if it is large and the task is complex. These structures may be temporary, i.e. for the duration of the exercise, or permanent. If the group in question is a permanent or continuing one, with individuals joining and leaving it, it may well be part of a larger organisation. In

which case, the organisation as a whole or your predecessor
as leader, may have already made sub-groups with leaders.
An infantry platoon, divided into sections, is a good example.
You may wish to maintain that ready-made structure, or introduce changes. The essence of organising at this level is to
break up the group into smaller sub-groups and to appoint
leaders who are responsible to you.

This will give you a second communications system. The
first is the method of talking to the whole group yourself and
listening to what they say – two-way, face-to-face communication. The content will include purpose, policies, progress
and people. The advantage of this method is that it is not
liable to the communication failures which occur when you
are passing messages to another person via a third (and fourth
and fifth . . .) party. But it is time consuming. Much, but not
all, of this communication work can be delegated to sub-
leaders. A good and well-trained sub-leader will not only pass
on and interpret messages accurately, but will also report back
to you clearly and concisely the reactions, constructive ideas
or suggestions which arose in his sub-group meeting on such
areas as:

how to do the *task* more effectively
how we can work better as a *team*
how each *individual* can contribute his greatest effort

The structure not only gives you a second communication
system, it also provides you with another option in your
decision making and problem solving strategy. You can now
put a problem or ask for proposed courses of action or solutions to your inner leadership team of sub-group leaders
rather than to the group as a whole. In choosing which of
these two methods for decision making to use, it is important
to be flexible according to the needs of the situation, the size
and character of the group and the kind of decision involved.

If your group is a large one (20 upwards) it is essential to
sub-divide it and appoint (or allow the members to elect)
leaders responsible to you, otherwise the individual needs
described elsewhere in this book are not going to be met. You
want each of your sub-leaders to involve their people in the
task, develop a team approach and to inspire, encourage and
control individuals as necessary. The more the sub-groups
can take on these functions themselves, with the minimum of

supervision, the better. But that, paradoxically, requires good leadership from you and their sub-group leader.

An experiment in the ham-cutting section at Plumrose Meats in Denmark in 1978 proves the value of small groups. There was a long line layout and short job cycles. Possible changes were discussed at section meetings for two weeks by 6 out of the 42 ham-cutters. As a result they proposed smaller groups of 6 to 8 people. The idea spread through the whole section and they resolved to work in five small groups with a co-ordinator who met a representative from each group. Productivity increased by 15 per cent. A questionnaire survey showed a favourable response and an interest in making further improvements.

Small group leader

Briefly, it was found that absenteeism and high labour turnover occurred predominantly amongst those workers who did not make a team, who had not managed to fit into any group (either because of personal peculiarities or, more usually, because they had not been given the opportunity to do so).

Having no social background, they had no feelings of loyalty and took little interest in what went on around them in the factory. On the other hand, investigation of a work team which had a production record 25 per cent above the average for the firm, showed up some of the factors which lead to good morale in the workshop. This group of men was recognised by the other workers as being somewhat clannish in that its members felt themselves to be superior to other groups – that is to say they showed loyalty and pride of membership. The foreman of the department where the group was employed was a busy man and rarely visited it, while his senior assistant visited it only once a day. All the work was in charge of a man who had no official standing whatever, but was the natural leader of the team.

This man had both the time in that he was not distracted by the necessity of dealing with technical problems, and the ability to concentrate on group solidarity. He handled this problem in the following manner: all new employees were introduced to the other members of the team and placed with those who seemed likely to make congenial associates; later, they were taken to the end of the assembly line to see where the part being made in the department fitted into the finished article. All complaints were dealt with at once by the leader, but if they were beyond his powers to handle he referred them to higher authority. The individual workers were in these ways given significance (they saw how their job fitted into the whole), comradeship (in being members of a team), and an awareness of being fairly treated.[1]

ORGANISING THE ORGANISATION

This may sound a rather meaningless sub-heading. After all, the organisation is by definition the end result of the function of organising. It is finished, complete and unalterable. Of course it is none of those things in reality, but we tend to make assumptions that it is so. An organisation is indeed sometimes the product of another person's organising activity. 'An institution is the lengthened shadow of one man', said Emerson. These days it is more likely to be a committee who did the organising. Some old and venerable kinds of organisations, like churches and armies, have structures which have lasted centuries modified but essentially unchanged. The fact that they have withstood the test of time may well be evidence that they are sound, but you cannot take that for granted. Whether the structure you are working in is the product of a single leader, a committee or a tradition, you should not assume that it is perfect either in the sense of being completely finished or in the sense of being without serious fault or blemish. For it is *people* who did the organising, and they are always fallible. They may have organised, for instance, with a particular interpretation of the enduring purpose in mind, or in light of a given technology, or assuming a certain level of education or training among members of the organisation. These *situational* factors are changing and therefore as a leader in an organisation you will need to examine the function of organising in one way or another.

Assuming that the organisation is not as hard as concrete but is organic, growing and developing or contracting according to the situation, your organising ability will be constantly in play introducing changes or modifications in the system or ways of doing things. From time to time it is advisable to carry out a survey of the structure of the organisation – its bony skeleton. You do not want to make changes in this basic structure too often, for no organisation (like the individual person) can stand too much change all at once. If you make a major organisational change, and get it wrong, you are stuck with the consequences for the next five years – longer, maybe, if it is a very big organisation. So it is important to get it right. Here management consultants can be useful. Just as building surveyors help you to assess what needs to be done when you buy a new house, so a good management consultant

can cast a professional eye over your organisation and suggest
the necessary changes.

Alternatively, you might prefer to carry out such a survey
yourself. Providing you take the three-circles model as your
guide you can undertake this structural survey without too
much difficulty, especially if you set up a small but representative committee to work with you. The key is to ask your-
selves the right questions; see Fig. 12.1 and Fig. 12.2 for
some suggestions.

Fig. 12.1

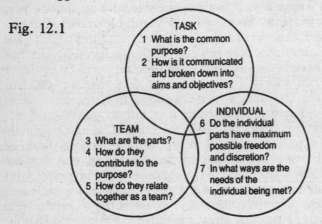

Surveying Your Organisation	
Question	Notes
1 What is the common purpose?	Besides studying statements of purpose look at what the organisation is actually doing. How does it spend its time and money?
2 How is it communicated and broken down into aims and objectives?	This should lead you into the communication and decision making processes, vital areas in any organisation
3 What are the parts?	Identify the main groups and subgroups. These are often divided between line (or operations) and staff (or functions) e.g. personnel. How many levels of leaders are there?

Fig. 12.2

Question	Notes
4 How do they contribute to purpose?	If they do not make a significant contribution they should not be there
5 How do they relate together as a team?	Does tribal war exist between departments, or do they co-operate harmoniously together? How well do they communicate on a lateral basis?
6 Do the individual parts have maximum possible freedom and discretion?	Is decision making pushed down as far as it will go, or is it heavily centralised? Do departments or units have sufficient freedom to use their initiative and creativity?
7 In what ways are the needs of the individual being met?	That will take you into systems of remuneration, personnel, and trade union activity
8 Do the circles sufficiently overlap?	You will soon find out how far the circles overlap in the minds of employees. Is the overlap sufficient to provide and maintain high morale in spite of difficulties?
9 How are tensions between them resolved?	That will take you into the consultative system, disciplinary procedures and the methods for dealing with disputes

Fig. 12.2 (continued)

You can begin your survey either at the bottom and work upwards, or at the top and work downwards. When I carried out such organisation surveys on the Dioceses of York and Chichester as a management consultant, I was able to start at the top because the Archbishop of York and the Bishop of Chichester respectively had commissioned me to do the survey. I saw myself as helping them and the senior leaders in the dioceses to perform for themselves the function of organising within the real (as compared to the assumed) constraints of the situation. For instance, I began by asking the Archbishop of York (Dr. Donald Coggan, later Archbishop of Canterbury) to let me have his statement of the purpose of the diocese in one sentence on a piece of paper, which he duly did. At a meeting over tea in the Athenaeum I can recall asking him 'Who are you accountable to?' He looked upwards!

Starting at the top

Jethro may be claimed as the patron saint of all management consultants! He certainly gave his son-in-law Moses some good advice on the need for an accountable structure. One day, while the tribes of Israel were in the desert, he saw Moses sitting alone with people standing around him from morning till evening, counselling them and solving disputes.

'This is not the best way to do it', said Jethro. 'You will only wear yourself out and wear out all the people who are here. The task is too heavy for you; you cannot do it by yourself. Now listen to me...' Jethro told him that he must remain the people's representative before God and to instruct them in the principles of how to behave and what to do. 'But you must yourself search for capable, God-fearing men among all the people, honest and incorruptible men, and appoint them over the people as officers over units of a thousand, of a hundred, of fifty or ten. They shall sit as a permanent court for the people; they must refer difficult cases to you but decide simple cases themselves. In this way your burden will be lightened, and they will share it with you. If you do this, God will give you strength, and you will be able to go on. And, moreover, this whole people will here and now regain peace and harmony'. Moses, who is described elsewhere as a 'very meek man', listened to his father-in-law and did all that he suggested.

Whether you start at the top and work downwards, or vice versa, it is important to be systematic about it. You are trying to see how the pieces of the jigsaw fit together at present, and to collect and collate ideas on how a better structure and method of working together might look.

At the lowest level you should search out the answers to the question: 'How large or small should the primary group or groups be in this industry?' A good guideline is to establish how many people one person can supervise in light of the factors shown in Fig. 12.3.

The Roman Army, like the Israelites, operated with a primary group of ten soldiers led by a *decanus* (hence our word 'dean'). A football and cricket team consists of 11 players. Jesus recruited 12 disciples, but they tended to break up into two sub-groups in dispute with each other, and one of them (lack of attention to individual needs?) betrayed him. However simple the task in technological terms, the span of control should probably not exceed 20 people. That means the num-

Size of Working Group	
Factor	Questions and Notes
Task/technology	How far does the work of subordinates interlock and need co-ordination? Quantity, variety and weight of matters for decision which are fed by subordinate to leader. Technical complexity and uncertainty usually narrows spans of control.
Communications	How geographically or physically dispersed are the subordinates or activities? What level of communication does the organisation expect from leader and subordinates?
Motivation and autonomy	How far do subordinates want to carry out the mutual integration themselves? Are they trained for such team-work?
Competence of leaders	A good leader can lead larger groups. But what are his other commitments? Does the leader have strong staff or specialist support?

Fig. 12.3

ber who are directly responsible to any given leader, and who therefore constitute his team.

James Keiller & Sons Limited is a manufacturing company with a factory in Dundee employing 400 people. Originally there was a broad supervisory structure with one superintendent responsible for approximately 30 people, running complex machines under the great pressures. About two years ago (in 1978) the company selected six employees in each group of 30 and appointed them working chargehands after first defining the job, giving them a differential of 12½ per cent and making each one responsible for five to six people running an individual plant and cost centre. These men were made entirely responsible for the production process in their own plant. At the other end of the management spectrum the company redefined the superintendent's role.

This same principle was then applied to maintenance staff. Traditionally maintenance had been an operation which took over when the machines stopped. Under the new structure four working chargehands were appointed for groups of five to six for each shift in each plant area. Although more men came into production maintenance the objective was much more to keep the lines running without breakdown rather than repair them after they had broken down. This system was run in parallel with that in the production area. All working chargehands were given an initial three- to four-day supervisory skills course and the company is going to build on this training.

Response to this reorganisation was very good. Employees reacted very well, breakdowns were minimised, the general working atmosphere greatly improved and people feel they know who is their boss. There has been a substantial improvement in productivity. In the past they had never been able to make their production targets. Now they are achieving them and able to consider increasing work volume.

If groups are to be kept small enough to manage effectively and for the leader to create team spirit and to inspire and influence each individual, there will be cases where there may not be enough for the leader to do. For example, in a garage what does the supervisor do when his 15 or 20 drivers are out on delivery? The best answer seems to be to use a senior driver, who will do the job himself for part of the time and carry out the leadership job in the rest. In the past, such working leaders have been greatly discouraged, especially on the factory floor, because they were inclined to spend too much time on the familiar technical job and not enough time standing back in order to perform the functions of leadership. But that is not an insuperable problem, given proper training. A bricklayer or carpenter foreman on a building site often works in this way with two or three other workmen.

There is a tendency higher up in an organisation to have too few people reporting to the next level. People who work in the middle levels of an organisation become aware that one of the reasons they do not give of their best is that the man above them is often doing their job for them. Partly this is due to the fact that each level does not have enough people reporting to them. (You may have noticed in reading the box on page 148 that Jethro divided the hundred into two groups of fifty, so that the man in charge there had only two men reporting to him – not enough. I like to think that is why 'Moses set his father-in-law on his way, and he went back to his own country'.)

If you have only two people reporting to you, it is perfectly possible, if you work hard, to do their jobs for them. But if you have 7 or 8 people reporting to you, the structure is encouraging you to delegate or collapse. As a rule of thumb, aim to build a structure of working groups composed of between 5 and 15 people. Such a policy will insure you against the common mistake of building into the structure too many levels of leadership or management. As Albert Einstein said, 'Everything should be made as simple as possible – but not simpler'.

A chemical company employs 588 people. The managing director has seven people reporting to him, and each of those has seven responsible to them. At the lowest level there are 12 people in each work group. That means only *three* levels of leadership.

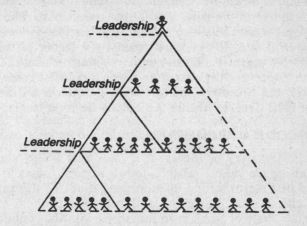

Fig. 12.4 Three Levels of Leadership

The organisational structure is the bony skeleton of the organisation. It should be functional in terms of the purpose, so that it adequately supports the muscle power and a robust communication system. Simplicity must be a hallmark at every level. Finally, it will only work if its cells and organs are free and flexible enough to be realigned at short notice to meet the challenges of a rapidly changing environment.

It is important always to keep coming back to *purpose*. A hospital exists to make sick people better, whatever ends are pursued by some of the staff working there. There is always a truth about why organisations are there – or what they should be doing – but it is often a great intellectual struggle to achieve and maintain clarity on the matter. This is especially true in a rapidly changing social, technological and economic situation. Changes in the methods or means by which the purposes are achieved are then demanded. Sometimes they call into question the fundamental purpose of the organisation.

It follows that if you are unable to define the purpose or to formulate any vision for the organisation, you will not be able to appraise its present structure or embark upon any meaningful organisational development. It often requires considerable courage, decisiveness and determination to set about re-organising to achieve the purpose more effectively in the present and in the future. Organisations tend to resist change. They like to live in the past, usually the recent past. The need for group cohesiveness – to remain together just as we are – is a powerful one. It can work against the leader as well as for him. No organisation can handle too much change all at once. The leader as chief executive needs a political sense to bring about the necessary changes with the minimum disruption, but if he does not tackle the agenda he is no leader.

A GOOD LEADER DELEGATES

From the story of Moses, it is clear that delegating and organising are closely related. Jethro advised Moses to delegate and that meant setting up an organisation. To delegate means to give a subordinate the authority and freedom to handle certain matters on his own initiative, with the confidence that he can do the job successfully. It is not to be confused with abdication.

| Delegation | Telling him results required and giving him the authority – "Do it your way and ask for help if required " |
| Abdication | Abdicating responsibility for the job – 'Do it any way you like but don't ask for help if it goes wrong' |

Sometimes people assume that an individual (or an organisation) can delegate more just at will. But delegation can only happen effectively, for example, if the right staff have been selected and trained for the job. For delegation to happen an

Leadership and Innovation

A company must balance the needs of all interested parties yet provide a satisfying and dignified life for its employees. In 1968 the labour turnover at Torslanda, Volvo's traditional factory, was 52 per cent. The 'average' worker thus felt the need to change jobs every two years. 'To me', says the company's president, Pehr G. Gyllenhammar, 'this seems horrifying'. Eliminating the root cause of boredom, he concludes, asks for a completely new approach to production and organisation, so that 'work' must be adapted to people, not people to machines'. A chance to put this philosophy into practice came with the building of a new factory at Kalmar. A revolutionary design established 500 production people into 25 groups, each group expert on a sub-assembly electrical system, or instrumentation, or interiors. The team organises its own work methods, is responsible for its own inspection and controls its own work pace. Work is brought to the team by computer controlled carriers. These can also be controlled manually by the team.

Kalmar acted as a catalyst for other plants including the 8,000 strong Torslanda factory. The pattern of gradual evolution established there repeated itself at other plants.

Gyllenhammar reflects here upon the leadership needed in industry, especially if meaningless work is to be outlawed.

'Leadership is giving support, explanations, and interpreting information so employees can understand it. Leadership is developing consensus. Leadership is sometimes the ability to say 'stop', to draw a line, to take the heat out of a conflict, to conclude a debate and get down to negotiations. Leadership is having the courage to put a stake on an idea, and risk making mistakes. Leadership is being able to draw new boundaries, beyond the existing limits of ideas and activities. Only through this kind of leadership can we keep our institutions from drifting aimlessly, to no purpose.

It sometimes scares me that what we do in Volvo is presented to others as an innovation, because this demonstrates, after all, how little has been done in work organisation. Companies spend almost endless hours trying to provide change, incentive, interest, involvement, and motivation for top executives, yet almost no time is spent in looking at the rest of the work force in the same way. Until now, managers have not found it necessary. We are still in the era that Adam Smith described so many years ago, where 'a worker gives up his ease, his liberty and his happiness when he goes into industry'.

If we can give the worker back his ease, his liberty and his happiness, or at least provide conditions under which he can find them for himself, I believe we will come closer to a healthy, human, "postindustrial" society.'[2]

organisation needs to pursue definite policies over selection, training, appraising or receiving performance and career planning.

Remember that you should not delegate unless you are willing to give the person concerned the necessary authority to do the job, matched with your supportive trust in him. Be available to discuss progress or help with any problems the subordinate cannot deal with himself. Grip your desk hard and do not interfere! Accept the fact that the job will be done differently from the way that you would have done it, but still fall within the bounds of success. Such effective delegation serves a two-fold purpose: it frees you for constructive work on larger projects, and it is a necessary technique for furthering the growth and development of subordinates. Make sure that the person knows what results are expected of him and that he is on his own and is accountable for full performance.

RESTRUCTURING INDIVIDUAL JOBS

A possible object for your organising ability or skill is the jobs that individuals are doing. Are they unnecessarily boring, dull or monotonous? It is vital to consult the person concerned here, because the profile of individual needs is as unique as a set of fingerprints. What seems repetitive to you may be reassuringly safe to someone else. Intelligence varies widely, and an apparently boring and mundane job can seem extremely interesting and responsible to a given individual doing it. To you and me, a hundred sheep all look the same but to the good shepherd they are all individuals.

ORGANISING YOURSELF

Sure signs of whether or not you are capable of executing the function of organising lie in your own life. Recently I had supper with a managing director; you could tell by his vegetable garden that he could organise.

The crucial sign is whether or not you are good at organising your own time. It is essential for the leader to make time to think, both about the present and the future. That means in the first place an awareness of the value of time and the economical use of it. 'Ask me for anything', Napoleon used to say, 'except for time'. He knew that he had only twenty-four hours a day like anyone else, but he used time more effectively. 'If you can fill the unforgiving minute, with sixty seconds worth of distance run . . .'

One method of developing your awareness and skill in time management is to keep a detailed diary of how you are spending your time. Often this reveals that relatively little time is being given to the key activities of leadership and communication, let alone thinking about decisions or problems. People dropping in during the morning, chatting or drinking coffee, or indiscriminate telephone calls can take up half your time. At the end of the day you go home with that uncomfortable feeling you have not really achieved anything.

Making Time to Think

What advice can be offered to a leader? He must discipline himself and lead a carefully regulated and ordered life. He must allow a certain amount of time for quiet thought and reflection; the best times are in the early morning, and in the evening. The quality, good or bad, of any action which is to be taken will vary directly with the time spent in thinking; against this, he must not be rigid; his decisions and plans must be adaptable to changing situations. A certain ruthlessness is essential, particularly with inefficiency and also with those who would waste his time. People will accept this, provided the leader is ruthless with himself . . .

Most leaders will find there is so much to do and so little time to do it; that was my experience in the military sphere. My answer to that is not to worry; what is needed is a quiety contemplation of all aspects of the problem, followed by a decision—and it is fatal to worry afterwards.[3]

Field Marshal Viscount Montgomery

Here are some practical suggestions to help you to organise your own personal work and the way you spend your time more effectively. Check yourself against this ten-point programme once a month for the next six months.

1 *Develop a new personal sense of time*
   Do not rely on memory: record where your time goes

2 *Plan ahead*
   Making plans on how you are going to spend your time a day, a week, a month, a year ahead. Plan in terms of opportunities and results, priorities and deadlines.

3 *Make the most of your best time*
   Programme important tasks for the time of day you function best. Have planned quiet periods for creative thinking.

4 *Capitalise on marginal time*
Squeeze activities into the minutes you spend waiting for a
train or between meetings.

5 *Avoid clutter*
Try re-organising your desk for effectiveness. Sort papers
into categories according to action priorities. Generate as
little paper as possible yourself.

6 *Do it now*
'Procrastination is the thief of time'
'My object was always to do the business of the day in the
day' (Wellington)

7 *Learn to say No*
Do not let others misappropriate your time.
Decline tactfully but firmly to avoid over-commitment.

8 *Use the telephone as a time-saving tool*
Keep telephone calls down to minimum length.
Screen telephone interruptions.

9 *Delegate*
Learn to delegate as much as possible.

10 *Meetings*
Keep them short.
Sharpen your skills as a chairman.
Cut out unnecessary meetings.

SUMMARY

Organising is the function of arranging parts into a working
order. 'Structure is a means for attaining the objectives and
goals of an institution', writes Peter Drucker. This is no more
than another application of the three-circles model. At group
level you may have to organise for results by setting up sub-
groups. At organisation level, however, the principle may
mean introducing structural changes to respond to changes in
the task, technology or the environment. This section contains
a guide for carrying out a survey of your own organisation,
based upon commonsense principles. Bringing about the
changes will, of course, require considerable powers of leadership, therefore to be effective as a leader you should be able
to organise your own work. You should become especially
good at managing your time, for it is your most precious
resource.

Discretionary Time

The executive who records and analyses his time and then attempts to manage it, can determine how much he has for his important tasks. How much time is there that is 'discretionary', i.e. available for the big tasks that will really make a contribution?

It is not going to be a great deal no matter how ruthlessly the executive prunes time-wasters.

Whenever I see a senior executive asserting that more than half his time is under his control, and is really discretionary time which he invests and spends according to his own judgment, I am reasonably certain that he has no idea where his time goes. Senior executives rarely have as much as one quarter of their time truly at their disposal and available for the important matters, the matters that contribute, the matters they are being paid for. This is true in any organization — except that in the government agency the unproductive time demands on the top people tend to be even higher than they are in other large organisations.

The higher up an executive, the larger will be the proportion of time that is not under his control and yet not spent on contribution. The larger the organization, the more time will be needed just to keep the organization together and running, rather than to make it function and produce.

The effective executive therefore knows that he has to consolidate his discretionary time. He knows that he needs large chunks of time and that small driblets are no time at all. Even one quarter of the working day, if consolidated in large time-units, is usually enough to get the important things done. But even three quarters of the working day are useless if they are only available as fifteen minutes here or half an hour there.

The final step in time management is therefore to consolidate the time that record and analysis show as normally available and under the executive's control.

Time is the scarcest resource; and unless it is managed, nothing else can be managed. The analysis of one's time, moreover, is the one easily accessible and yet systematic way to analyse one's work and to think through what really matters in it.

'Know Thyself', the old prescription for wisdom, is almost impossibly difficult for mortal men. But everyone can follow the injunction 'Know Thy Time' if he wants to, and be well on the road toward contribution and effectiveness.[4]

Peter Drucker

CHECKLIST: ORGANISING

Organising is an important function in meeting all three circles. Check your organising ability in the following areas.

Group	Yes	No
Is the size of the working group correct and are the right people working together?	☐	☐
Is there a need for sub-groups to be constituted?	☐	☐
Are there regular opportunities or procedures for genuine consultation with the group before taking decisions affecting them, eg. decisions relating to work plans and output, work methods and standards, work measurement, overtime working?	☐	☐

Organisation		
Are you clear on the purpose of the organisation and how the various parts of it work together to achieve that end?	☐	☐
Is there an effective system for staffing the organisation and training? Is there a fair dismissal procedure?	☐	☐

Do you carry out regular surveys of the organisation to check
- size of all working groups   . . . .
- number of leadership levels   . . . .
- growth of unnecessary complexity   . . . .
- line and staff co-operation   . . . .
- communication systems working properly   . . . .

Yourself		
Are there ways in which you could organise your personal and working life, e.g. where you live, in order to be a more effective leader?	☐	☐
Do you delegate sufficiently?	☐	☐

Have you identified at least three steps you can take in order to become a better organiser of your time?
1
2
3

13 Setting An Example

As a leader you cannot help setting an example – the question is whether it will be a good or a bad one. If you are setting a good example people will tend not to be too aware of it, but they will certainly notice and comment upon a bad example. 'I cannot hear what you are saying, for what you are is thundering in my ears', as the African proverb puts it.

Example is important because people take in information more through their eyes than their ears. What they see you do is far more powerful than what they hear you say. The basic principle is that word and example should always go together. They should support each other. If they conflict, you must expect people to follow your example and not your precept: 'Don't do as I do – do as I say': those words should never pass the lips of a true leader, except in so far as they acknowledge that he is aspiring towards a common high standard, and – being human – is all too aware of his own shortcomings. People will respect you if you try to set the right example, even if you fall short on occasions.

IN THE TASK AREA

A root meaning of leadership is leading in the sense of literally going out in front of the others. A person who does that, an Alpine guide, for example, is using his own body to convey to the followers in what direction they should be travelling. When we widen the reference to non-physical situations, the leader is still the person who gives others a sense of direction in a given field by his own behaviour. Leadership implies the personal willingness to go out in front – accepting the risks involved – in order to ensure that your team go in the right direction and at the right speed. To continue the analogy, if you are too far ahead of the group – too advanced in your thinking – you run the risk of losing contact with them altogether. If you are too far behind, however, you may find yourself saying, like a politician in the French Revolution: 'There goes my group – I must follow them'.

Just how much of an example you should set by personally doing the work yourself depends upon your level of leadership. At the lower levels you should expect to lead by doing the job – or part of it at least – yourself in the way you expect it to be done. But the other functions of leadership, notably controlling and co-ordinating, should take priority if there is any conflict over how your time should be spent.

Leading by Example

Preparation and planning are among the most important facets, I feel, of any kind of leadership. Having worked out a plan one can then put it to the team, always being prepared to be flexible in the face perhaps of better ideas. The other vital thing I feel is that your fellow team members must respect your own devotion to the interests of the expedition as a whole as opposed to your own personal interests. You can only expect loyal acceptance of your decisions if you are genuinely putting your fellow team members first rather than yourself. The final factor is that you undoubtedly have to be prepared to work considerably harder than any of the people you are leading. There are many occasions when you need to lead by example and yet, at the same time, one must be careful not to get bogged down in a series of minor chores that nobody else wants to do, so that you cannot fulfil your main function of running the expedition as a whole.

Chris Bonnington

In the military field this aspect of leadership tends to be crystal clear. The platoon commander is expected to lead his platoon from the front; the squadron leader flies his own fighter as well as controlling the squadron. At a certain level, however, the military commander does not lead the attack in person. 'We shall be right behind you on the day, sir,' said one eager sergeant to General Slim in Burma. 'Make no mistake, Sergeant', replied Slim, 'when the day comes you will be several miles in front of me!'

Does the senior leader then stop leading by example? Not necessarily. The fact that he has led himself in the basic task is itself an important factor in winning the respect of subordinates. It has the added practical advantage that they know such a leader will not ask them to do what he would not be willing to do himself – or to have done in the past. If he is not willing to do the job himself he can hardly command others to do it.

At the age of 21 years I was working as a deckhand in a Hull fishing trawler. The mate in charge of the deckhands was a large bully of a man with a chip on his shoulder, for he had recently been a skipper but lost his ticket through incompetence. One afternoon, in a winter storm near Iceland, he told one of the men to shin up the mast and adjust an unsafe navigation light. 'Not bloody likely', said the man, looking at the kicking mast and hissing waves. 'You do it, Bill', thundered the mate to another deckhand. 'Not me', replied Bill with a shrug. The mate began to shout and swear at us all. Attracted by the commotion on deck, the skipper came down from the bridge. 'What's up?', he asked. The mate told him. 'Why don't you go up yourself?' the skipper said to the mate, looking him in the eye. Silence. 'Right, I'll do it myself', said the skipper, and began to pull off his oilskin. He meant it too. At once three or four men stepped forward and volunteered, for we had no desire to lose our navigator overboard.

Which was the true leader – the mate or the skipper?

Even at the more senior levels of leadership it is sometimes possible for the leader to give what might be called a symbolic example. When Napoleon found a sentry asleep one night he took up the man's musket and stood guard himself for a few hours. Occasionally a senior leader can 'lend a hand', working beside his people for an hour or two. Such gestures can have an electric effect upon men in direct ratio to the rank or seniority of the leader concerned. The grapevine, which can be a positive as well as a negative factor in large organisations, will carry the good news around. 'Did you know what I saw the other day? Mr. Jenkins, the managing director, took off his coat and helped clean out No. 3 boiler and then had tea with the lads. He must have been there about an hour'.

At this point the hackles rise on some senior manager's back 'Surely it isn't the job of a managing director to clean out a boiler!' Of course it isn't. But men are touched by the imaginative gesture. Leadership involves the ability to inspire. A gram of example is worth a kilogram of exhortation. Sometimes such a symbolic act can serve to remind a group or an organisation of the busic meaning of leadership. It is as if the leader is saying 'I should like to be with you all more often, especially when there is a dirty or arduous job to be done,

---

Admiral of the Fleet Sir Michael Le Fanu

Le Fanu was the least orthodox leader to reach high rank in the Royal Navy since the Second World War. He had a sense of humour which he put creatively to work. One of those who served under him wrote that his 'natural concern for all made it a sure thing there was nothing you would not do for him. He was a born leader, a man's man, he had style – and terrific compassion'. In 1967 he was Commander-in-Chief of the British forces in the troubled land of Aden. Where possible the red-haired admiral led by example.

Whenever he could persuade his staff to let him take the risks involved, he put in an appearance at the front line – he would suddenly arrive by helicopter and join a patrol on a cordon and search operation and make his presence known wherever things were difficult. Out in the Radfan, the men of 45 Commando, Royal Marines, had been on their feet in disagreeable circumstances for several days when Michael came to see them. Their Chaplain, Ray Roberts, dressed in crumpled denims and not looking in the least like a Naval Chaplain, was staggered when Michael walked up to him in the desert and continued a conversation they'd had five years earlier.

According to Roberts, it was on a visit to the Radfan (and not on the dockside) that one of the best known Le Fanu incidents occurred. On one occasion, wearing his khaki uniform with four stars pinned into the shirt peaks, he gave a hand to an airman who had a lot of stores to unload from an aircraft. The airman had not recognised the face or understood the unusual badges of his companion, but finding that the older man was not doing terribly well, exhorted him with the deathless injunction, 'Come on Ginge, get a bloody move on!' 'What did you do?' Roberts asked him later. 'Exactly what I was told to', Michael replied, 'I got a move on!'

In 1970 Le Fanu was appointed Chief of the Defence Staff but he was compelled to resign by ill-health before he could take up the appointment.

As a footnote, I may add that I met Admiral Sir Michael Le Fanu briefly at a wedding reception for the first and last time, for it was a week before he died. Apart from his evident friendliness, I was enormously impressed by his lively interest in leadership. Perhaps the greatest example he set to all aspiring leaders lay in his willingness to go on thinking about leadership right up to the last week of his life.[1]

but my other responsibilities just do not allow me too. At least what I have done this afternoon is a token that I mean what I say'.

IN TEAM AND INDIVIDUAL CIRCLES

The importance of setting an example in setting, maintaining, or altering group standards has been touched upon already. Punctuality is an obvious instance. Whatever you require the group to do, you should be prepared to do yourself. If you want each member to help the others with their work you can

---

Breaking down status barriers

Peter Prior became Chairman and Chief Executive of H. P. Bulmer Ltd., the Hereford cider-makers, in 1973.

In Bulmer we have taken many initiatives to improve communication and to foster the 'whole team' idea, and our success is measurable. To persuade shopfloor workers that we regarded them just as highly as office workers some nine years ago we discontinued the practice of clocking on and off; timekeeping has in fact improved.

Another initiative, possibly flamboyant but nevertheless effective, is that I, and some of the other directors, have regularly spent days working on the shopfloor, not because we can do the job as well as the regular operators, but rather to indicate that we are not a company divided. The trade unions have not objected to this approach and it would be very nice if they could take the bull by the horns and promote it elsewhere. After all, in the long term the objectives of management and shopfloor must be identical, for only through co-operation can valid long-term objectives actually be attained. Confrontation, however emotionally satisfying in the short term, is never practical politics in the long term. Participation by employees in the management of the organisation which employs them is co-operation in its purest form – in the wealth creation process which is as vital to the firm as it is to Britain.

The creation of more wealth each year, the increase in our national production, the ability to do just a little better than our competitors overseas, all these will benefit the shopfloor proportionately more than they are likely to benefit managers or shareholders. But to achieve this demands a wholesale change of attitude in order to break down the barriers which prevent companies from working as a united, productive team.

Only top management, however, can take the decisions that will put their organisations on such a path, because effective change can only come from the very top. Personal leadership from the top can create a receptive environment in which teamwork can truly flourish right down the line. The old barriers can at last be replaced with genuine trust.[2]

best convey that by doing it yourself. The norms of human relations – listening, respecting, communicating and caring – can all be best conveyed by example. When Jesus wanted to impress upon his disciples that as leaders they should be prepared to meet the needs of individuals, he did not give them a long lecture on social psychology. Instead he took a bowl, jug of water and a towel, knelt down and washed their dusty feet. By thus performing the functions of a lowly household servant he was also teaching them the need for humility as Christian leaders, a virtue in stark contrast to the self-vaunting arrogance of the Gentile kings and lords.

Example is contagious. It is action or conduct which induces imitation. Children are naturally imitative: it is the way they learn. As adults we retain that characteristic. In creating the right climate of purpose, unity and teamwork, how you bear yourself as leader can be decisive. 'You mention integrity as an important quality', a manager asked Lord Slim at a large conference for industrialists. 'Can you suggest how this quality can be spread in industry?' 'Yes, by example,' replied Slim.

There are not many chief executives in industry who are prepared to travel around their organisations incognito like Sir Michael Le Fanu, cheerfully accepting the directions of a foreman to load packing cases. Nor is there any evidence that Peter Prior's example of regularly working some days on the shopfloor or out on a delivery lorry is widely followed. But there are plenty of other ways of setting an example.

In 1981 the chief executive of one major company put pressure on his workforce to accept a pay offer of 3.8 per cent, while he himself took a 38 per cent rise. That same year, however, the 100 directors of Britain's biggest industrial company, ICI, sacrificed an 8.5 per cent pay rise because of the firm's poor profits performance. In view of ICIs 6,000 redundancies and poor trading conditions the directors agreed to give up the 8.5 per cent rise awarded to the firm's 78,000 UK employees. It was an unprecedented act in the company's history. 'The directors felt', explained an ICI spokesman, 'that they should make a positive gesture'. Other leading British firms do not seem to have followed ICIs example. Very few stuck to any form of pay freeze at top levels – despite demanding zero pay rises from their workers!

Good example, then, has creative power, especially if it involves an element of self-sacrifice. It can work in men's minds to alter their ways. That process may take time, but the leader whose example backs up his words puts himself in an unassailable position. No one can accuse him of hypocrisy – of preaching one thing and doing another.

He that gives good advice builds with one hand. He that gives good counsel and example builds with both. But he that gives good admonition and bad example, builds with one hand and pulls down with the other.

Francis Bacon

The principle of example is a challenging one, for it involves not only what you do but also who you are and how you live. It reminds you that leadership can never be a thing apart from the rest of your life. In practical terms your own example is the most powerful weapon at your command. As Dag Hammarskjold, Secretary General of the United Nations, wrote to himself one night in his diary:

Your position never gives you the right to command. It only imposes on you the duty of so living your life that others can receive your orders without being humiliated.

SUMMARY

'Leadership *is* example', wrote one officer cadet on his observation sheet after a two-week exercise while I was at Sandhurst. I have often reflected on his words. It seems to me that true leaders are linked by this principle that in some way or other they *set an example* – they *do* or *live* what they preach or require in others. This separates them from the mere talkers. Even communication is seldom just a matter of talking. It involves what is often called non-verbal communication. Example belongs in that category. It is relevant to the *task* circle, as the original meaning of leadership – going out in front – makes clear. Where that physical leading is not appropriate you can set an example, for instance by working hard or being accurate and well-informed. Example can help you to *build the team*, for you can illustrate by example the new standards you are introducing or changing. The *individual* who knows you or sees you from afar may be inspired to emulate you. You may need some creative imagination to apply this principle, but apply it you must if you are committed to becoming a better leader. If it calls for an element of self-denial or sacrifice on your part so much the better. That will almost certainly win a response.

CHECKLIST:
SETTING AN EXAMPLE

Which of these statements would you say most applies to you?:

People often comment on the good example you set in your work. You never ask others to do what you are not willing to do yourself. ....

Sometimes your bad example conflicts with all that we are trying to do here ....

You are not really aware of the importance of example and are unable to say what kind of one you are giving ....

On what occasion in the last month have you deliberately set out to give a lead by your example?

Did your action have any effect on the group or individual:

(a) immediately   Yes ☐   No ☐
(b) some days later   Yes ☐   No ☐

What specific problems in team maintenance area might you help to solve by giving a better personal example yourself?

(1)

(2)

If you are a senior leader or an appraiser of other leaders, have you mentioned to others the importance of example in leadership during the last three months?

         Yes ☐   No ☐

Using the 'brainstorming' approach (p. 89) see if you can produce three new – more creative – ways in which you and more senior leaders in the organisation might set an example. They should be ways not tried before.

Part Three
GROWING AS
A LEADER

Contrary to what some people seem to believe, there is no such thing as 'instant leadership'. It is not a collection of 'behaviours' or techniques you can acquire on a course. The eight functions and skills described in Part Two have to be developed over a period of time. They involve what you *are* and what you *know* as well as what you are able to *do*. Therefore you need to grow as a leader in a way which involves your leadership qualities, knowledge and skills. What are the conditions for that long-term growth? They lie partly in YOURSELF and partly in the ORGANISATION in which you work. Each of these two facets is the subject of a section that follows.

When you have finished reading and reflecting upon Part Three, and carefully and thoroughly completed the checklists it contains, you should be able:

1 to appreciate the conditions necessary in any ORGANISA-TION if those with leadership ability or potential are to be fully developed and used.
2 to set down on paper the rough draft of a LEADERSHIP SELF-DEVELOPMENT PROGRAMME covering the next five years.
3 to identify at least five short-term ACTION POINTS for improving your own leadership.

14 Does Your Organisation Develop Leaders?

'We are most interested in your ideas – and your practical work at Sandhurst and in industry. We should definitely like to emphasise the importance of leadership in management during the 1980s and are looking for ways to do it. Can you give us the names of any companies that have really done all that you think should be done?'

The senior personnel manager who asked me that question belonged to one of the largest companies in the United Kingdom. After a pause, I had to answer that I could not name one! Yes, there were hundreds of organisations sending managers on Action-Centred Leadership courses or running ACL extensively on an in-company basis. Yes, there were companies I could name who had first-rate top leaders, or good structures, or proper career development programmes. But I could not name *one* organisation that was doing it *all* right. No single company had really got the *whole* approach together.

Later, after more reflection, I held myself partly responsible for that fact. For I have never set down in a clear and easily accessible way the *organisational principles of developing leaders*.

If you happen to be a *chief executive* or a member of a board of directors, this section should speak directly to you, for it is your responsibility to develop the leadership the organisation needs in the present and future. If you are a *senior personnel adviser* you may find here the basis for a plan which you can submit.

If you are not at the top you should still read this section, if only in order to assess how far your organisation is shaping up to the challenge of leadership development, for your

A Historian Looks at Leadership

Given the course of English history, which I see as a quest for liberty, equality and personal responsibility, there is no hope that we will ever become good technological ants, loyal cogs in the organisation. We have to find an English road to salvation.

Now earlier in my talk I suggested that in modern industrialised society a leader needed both the raw quality of leadership – personal force and will – *and* complete technical mastery of the job itself. It would seem that British management is too often lacking in both. But then 'leadership' is not much talked about with regard to industry. 'Management' is the preferred word. 'Management studies' thrive. Is there here another source of trouble?

Note the entirely different resonances of these two phrases: 'trade-union leaders'; 'plant manager'. Try switching the epithets and you get even more clearly the difference between the resonances of the words: 'trade-union *manager*'. How funny it sounds! 'Plant leader' – the same. I think this sharply brings out that management and leadership are not at all the same thing. To my mind 'management' is concerned with the inanimate – material and financial resources, machinery, products, marketing. 'Leadership' is concerned with people; it is a psychological – or if you like, a spiritual – connection between human beings. Therefore, given the historical nature of our industrial population, more emphasis on 'management' and 'management training' will not cure our problems. To think in terms of 'managing' your fellow men is in any case to dehumanise both them and the relationship between you. This is shown by the very jargon of the 'behavioural sciences' – even as white rats.

We must think, then, in terms of 'leadership' – but a form of leadership still new to industry, even though much in the British tradition. The leader not as a *boss*, but as first among *equals*; seeking to bring out the full potential of those he works with; careful to carry them with him in all he seeks to do. He will lead not through rank or the weight of social position, but by virtue of superior intelligence and strength of personality; by virtue of being best at the job itself. He will devolve and share responsibility and decision as far as he can. He will need insight into his team-mates and their strengths and weaknesses. He will welcome ideas and suggestions from those who in a former dispensation might have been regarded as his inferiors. He will build a relationship of mutual trust.

However, such a style of leadership implies radical changes in the organisational framework of industrial life. For example, the final abolition of those outward forms which proclaim a distinction between boss and man, white collar and blue collar.

It may therefore be that our salvation as an industrial nation, as well as an immense step forward as a society, will lie in the coming at long last to every office and shopfloor of that English habit of cabinet government which first evolved in Downing Street two hundred and fifty years ago ... the free collaboration of *responsible individuals* in a common enterprise.[1]

Corelli Barnett

development only partly depends upon your inherent abilities and willingness to stretch yourself. You also have to be in the right situation at the right time. Just as a plant needs light, food and warmth, so you need certain conditions present in the organisation. A famous athletics coach used to say that 'champions were planted in the winter, tended in the spring, and blossomed in the summer'. Developing leaders is a similar process.

What, then, are these conditions that you should be seeking to create in your organisation so that it becomes a more fruitful source for practical leaders? There are ten such conditions or principles.

1 A strategy for leadership development

Organisations who mean business in this field will need to formulate a strategy for leadership development at board of director level or its equivalent.

'*Leadership* development. Surely you mean *management* development?'

That question underlies the need for the board of directors to set aside at least one whole day in order to discuss and formulate their policy in this respect, for there is much confusion between the terms 'leadership' and 'management'. Being a manager in industry or commerce certainly implies more than leadership, for the work or profession of management has its own body of knowledge. Leadership is an essential part of managing. It grows in importance as the 'human side of enterprise' becomes that much more significant. At general management level – as the specialist gives ground to the generalist – leadership should be seen as the core of the activity of managing.

After formulating a leadership development strategy the board of directors should ensure that:

(a) a high proportion of those working for the organisation know about it: *briefing*
(b) there are regular reviews of progress in implementing it: *evaluating*
(c) it is up-dated as new ideas or developments become available: *planning*

What should the elements of that strategy be? What are the principles the strategic thinkers must apply?

2 Selection

All organisations have methods of selecting their future leaders. Interviewing, combined with scrutiny of the written application form, *curriculum vitae* and references, are still the main methods employed.

It is surprising that no industrial or commercial organisations seem to have explored the possibility of adopting or adapting the group approach to leadership testing (see p. 26) in its entirety. Several organisations, however, have introduced leadership exercises into the selection procedures. There is scope for much more experiment along these lines.

All that such selection procedures will do is to identify young people in terms of their natural *potential* for enabling a group to achieve a common task, building or maintaining a team and meeting individual needs. It should encompass some estimate of their personality (including temperament), aptitudes and interests in relation to the working situation: the general nature of the task activity and the environment in which it has to be pursued.

Should psychological tests be used? My impression is that their use is declining in large organisations now. From the leadership angle, their danger is that they can be almost too effective in picking 'round pegs' for 'round holes', but this kind of matching ignores the dimension of change and the need for creative people in the organisation.

Recently a large conglomerate of firms invited me to take part in their annual conference for personnel managers. During the three days we spent together I was struck by their complacency. They had achieved a certain level in their 'personnel policies' as they called them. Welfare and benefits were good, but they were not interested in developing leadership. They seemed resigned to their faceless committee management. They lacked creative thinkers or creative innovation. By chance some twenty years ago I had come across their selection techniques. Psychologists tested applicants for two whole days. These tests certainly enabled them to choose good company men, who would fit into present job specifications and not rock the boat. But I wonder now if in that process they did not screen out *all* the creative people. Hence the seeds of the present problems were sown two decades ago.

It is in fact difficult to predict who will be the 'high-flyers' in leadership when the organisation is selecting managers from relatively young and inexperienced candidates. Good judges of character may be able to sense by intuition when they interview someone with this potential for great leadership. Often he may seem to be someone who does not fit the jobs available, for he will come into his own at a higher level, or perhaps in some situation in the future which the leaders of the organisation today have not even dreamt about. Among the young men and women recruited today will probably be those who will be required to lead the organisation in the year 2010. Just think for a moment of the changes they will have to cope with – and manage – in the decades before then. Just imagine the kind of leadership that will be needed when they eventually reach the top of your organisation in those days.

The leader as 'outsider'

As far as the leader is concerned, he is not one of a group; and if he is a true leader and not just a bell-wether, the lead sheep in a flock with a bell around its neck that the rest will follow, he never will belong. A leader is always something of an outsider. He must see over the heads of the group and beyond it. He has more 'stature' in the sense that one can measure the stature of a man by how far he sees. Very often leaders see so far that they are not recognised early. They are prophets whom lesser men fail to understand. It is only when the coincidence of vision and moment is right that what the leader has to say makes sense to lesser men.[2]

David Stinton

Selecting those with leadership potential is essential. They may not all be 'high-flyers', but then every organisation needs mostly mainstream leaders. The exceptionally gifted will tend to select themselves anyway. To whatever degree, however, that potential ability – functional and qualities – must be there. Even the best gardeners cannot turn a tulip into a rose by using good fertilizer.

3 Training for leadership

It is unfair, if not immoral, to give a person a leadership job without giving him some training for leadership. Yet hundreds of organisations do just that. It is unfair on that person, but it is even rougher for those whom he is expected to lead.

> Michael Jones is a brilliant metallurgist. Working hard in his university laboratory, employing x-ray crystallography techniques, he acquired a wide reputation and published many papers. Then, at the age of 50, he was appointed head of the Materials and Metallurgy Department at Stirlchester University. The academic staff, technicians and secretaries were soon writhing in discontent. 'He is no leader', one declared. But who was to blame? As Michael said, 'I have never had any training in leadership or management. It's too late to teach an old dog new tricks now'.

We should think of education or training for leadership as happening at different stages in a person's career. The foundations should have been laid before a person presents himself for a job involving the management of people – at school, in the family and in tertiary education (college, polytechnic, university or the national training schemes for young people who are unemployed or at work under the age of 20 years). Your organisation should take an active interest in these areas, just as a gardener should look to his seedbeds. For industry can contribute directly or indirectly to leadership development in schools and further education, as well as instituting appropriate programmes for its own young employees. An element of this active intervention into the social environment ought to feature in your strategy.

Training for leadership in the form of an ACL course or its equivalent should come shortly before or shortly after a person has been given a leadership job. There are pros and cons for both positions.

Before: Gives the person a sketchmap and guidelines.
               Reduces likelihood of serious mistakes.
               But no direct experience to relate to Functional Leadership theory.

After: Will bring leadership experience to the course.
               Has encountered difficulties, so very motivated to learn.
               But it may already be too late, at least for this job.

What does 'shortly' mean? Not more than six months either way, I would suggest.

The training course concerned, whether it is ACL-based or not, should have certain hallmarks or characteristics (see pp. 67–74). If it is done on an in-house or in-company basis, the course should be adapted to give it maximum relevance to the needs and character of the organisation.

The principle of training for leadership should apply right up to the top jobs. Many organisations have introduced ACL for first-line managers – foremen and supervisors – and for middle managers, but they neglect to provide advance leadership training in the form of seminars, conferences or individually-tailored programmes for senior managers and the board of directors.

4 A career development policy

One survey of 200 chief executives reveals that the average age when they entered senior management is 32 years. They achieved the top job at an average of 41. On the way up these 'high-flyers' had worked in more than eight different jobs in two or three different organisations.[3] Behind these facts we can glimpse an essential story, admittedly speeded-up in the case of budding chief executives but true for all who aspire to rise as leaders in organisations. It is the process by which a specialist becomes a generalist by planned career moves.

> The managing director of a bottling company mentioned in our conversation that he had recently moved his finance director and put him in charge of marketing and distribution. 'He should be challenging for my job soon', he added. 'He has what it takes, but he lacks experience of the business as a whole. He realises that, and we have agreed on this move as part of his development.'

The story or process of your career can be represented in the form of an hour-glass or egg-timer. As you move through the narrow neck of the glass you will begin to acquire the wider knowledge or experience of the purpose of the organisation as a whole, as compared to your specialised part or contribution within it. That career movement, however, sets up the need for training in leadership, communication and decision making where you are not the technical expert.

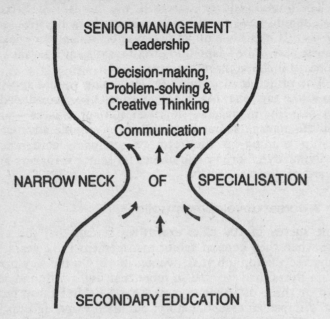

SENIOR MANAGEMENT
Leadership

Decision-making,
Problem-solving &
Creative Thinking

Communication

NARROW NECK   OF   SPECIALISATION

SECONDARY EDUCATION

Fig. 14.1 General Management Areas of Competence

Much has been spoken about the 'small is beautiful' concept in organisations. From the human angle there is indeed much to be said for working in small organisations or companies. Communication, for example, tends to be less of a problem, but the potential advantages of size are not only economic ones. They include the ability to offer people opportunities of developing and gaining experience in other divisions or companies within the group. Strangely enough, many very large organisations do not capitalise on this asset. They may move people within functions, e.g. finance, but they do not really cross-post them. Why, then, have a large organisation, you may ask.

If your organisation is getting it right it will not allow the leaders of tomorrow to stagnate in jobs. That does not mean they should be moved every year before their mistakes have a chance to catch up on them! There has to be time to achieve some objectives, to build up a 'track-record', but the emphasis should be upon onwards and upwards. That means wider knowledge, gained through working in a range of functional areas, on the staff as well as in line management. It may include secondments and periods away from the organisation altogether. This situational approach, however, should be coupled with a broadening and deepening of the manager's study of universal leadership. Without raising false expectations it is always right to explain to the person concerned precisely *why* the move is being proposed. Otherwise an appointment to manage your big plant in Siberia may look more like a punishment than an opportunity!

EXERCISE 12

The following matrix (Fig. 14.2) can be used to plot your own early and mid-career development. Additionally or alternatively, you can apply it in a mini-survey of any *five* people occupying positions of senior responsibility in your organisation. Each may have a different profile – discuss the pros and cons with them. Looking back, would they have preferred a different story?

Experience	Age 18–24	25–30	31–38	39–40
One function or specialism e.g. accountancy selling engineering				
Same function but in two organisations				
Two or more functions in (1) same organisation				
(2) different organisations				
General Manager, responsible for all functions in a given area				

Fig. 14.2 Career development matrix

5   Line managers as leadership mentors

If line managers are taking the three circles approach seriously they will accept that developing the individual includes developing his leadership potential. That involves far more than just sending the person concerned on an ACL-type course. It means trying to do 'on the job' leadership training. That involves the function of evaluating in the form of appraising the individual – identifying strengths and weaknesses, encouraging, advising and listening. An annual formal appraisal interview should be no more than a safety-net, a ratification of points discussed. If so, it need not last more than ten minutes.

Before and after a person goes on a leadership course he should be briefed and de-briefed by the person he reports to. The first talk is to establish clearly why the organisation thinks it worth spending their money and his time on the course. The person's training needs and the course objectives have to tie up. Afterwards the line manager will want to know his colleague's action points, so that he can help him to implement them. They may entail changes in the way the department is organised or run, which will need digesting – sometimes with a stiff gin.

If your line managers are themselves leaders of some stature, leading by example as well as precept, the young managers will be learning a great deal more from working with them, observing them and talking to them than they can ever put into words.

At a crisis in my youth, he taught me the wisdom of choice, to try and fail is at least to learn; to fail to try is to suffer the inestimable loss of what might have been'.[4]

If an organisation can promote respect and affection among its managers, then they will be far more likely to help each other to become more effective leaders.

6   Research and development

Like any other field, developing leadership has a certain amount of technical expertise to it. The text-books tend to be written in jargon. You need to have been around a certain time within that sphere before you can catch up with what is happening. Therefore, an organisation needs to have its specialist in leadership research and development. He should always be associated with a small group of line managers or their equivalents who have a more-than-average interest in the subject and who can be realistic.

Apart from looking at new ideas, courses and training aids such specialists might also be charged with evaluating the effectiveness of courses, training the trainers (who may be line managers) and advising the top management on the progress of their strategy.

7   Getting the structures right

Nothing causes more frustration or impedes leadership development than a poor organisational structure. As chief executive a key part of your leadership – the organising function at your level – must be devoted to getting the structure right. It will never be perfectly alright, but some organisations are definitely worse than others in this respect. Often you will be faced with an option of difficulties.

The Kindermere Healthcare Trust has grown in the last five years to 32 private hospitals, scattered throughout the United Kingdom. It now has 3000 employees. There are 32 matrons all reporting to one Chief Nursing Officer in London. Should KHT *regionalise* in order to create a smaller span of control? But to do so means introducing *another level of management*. What would you do?

What matters in organisational design is that it should be possible for the leaders to lead. That means that they should have the time to talk to their team and not be sentenced to solitary confinement behind a desk.

Organisational structure alone does not guarantee good leadership, but if it gets very out-of-date, top-heavy or lop-sided, it can make the work of leadership extremely difficult. Sometimes an organisation will then fall into a vicious circle. Conservative managers or leaders may maintain time-honoured structures despite the fact that they have become rigid or dys-functional. Those structures in turn attract or develop

> ### Making time to lead
>
> If I am to achieve a relationship with my colleagues which enables us all to give of our best there needs to be a limit to the number which directly report to me. A need to identify necessitates on both sides the giving of time. Time to understand the other person, find out what makes him tick, what are his strengths and weaknesses and whether there are short cuts in getting through to that person for the purpose of getting things done effectively. One of the great benefits of a well established relationship is that it reduces the need for lengthy dialogue although it does not and never should eliminate regular briefing sessions.
>
> Regrettably, we do not always have the time or, worse still, find the time to get to know many of our colleagues well enough to exercise this advantage. Leadership necessitates a two way acceptance of a special relationship; it has to be built on mutual trust and respect but it involves also a complex matrix of skills and sensitive perceptions, perhaps the most important of all, listening and hearing; the two are not necessarily synonymous. If I had to summarise what leadership means to me it would be the understanding and sharing of a common purpose – without that there cannot be effective leadership.
>
> *Ann Mansell,*
> *Chief Executive of Texales Ltd*

managers who cannot lead, and so it goes on. The remedy is to get the structure right and keep it in trim.

8 Self-development

Throughout this book I have assumed that you 'own' the problem of how to develop *your* leadership potential, so that it becomes real, effective and rewarding. The following chapter is entirely on that theme, but I believe that the organisation should have done that job for me, long before you picked up this book.

The benefit for an organisation in applying this principle is that it can enter into a *partnership* with its young leaders or leaders-to-be which is to their mutual advantage. The former can supply opportunities, training and encouragement, whereas the latter bring high motivation and the willingness to learn. Both have to be honest with each other in their relationship. In particular the organisation must strive to give its honest impressions, in the form of realistic feedback, of how far up the ladder of promotion a person is likely to rise. Has he the makings of a senior level leader? Those impressions may prove wrong, but they should be given.

The apparent disadvantage of such a policy, of course, is that the manager concerned may come to place his self-development as a leader in front of the needs of the organisation, but this drawback does not stand up to serious examination. Both the organisation and the individual concerned may agree that the right next opportunity is lacking, and so it makes sense to look elsewhere. Remember those 200 chief executives? On average they had worked for *two or more* organisations.

A good organisation will probably produce more leaders than it can use at senior level, for all pyramids narrow towards the top. 'Why should we train leaders for other companies?', one manager once asked me. Yet most organisations import leaders at one level or another and at certain times, and so they should be willing to export them as well. Besides, it is surely no bad thing to improve the whole industry or field of work by training some of its leaders.

9 Organisational climate

The prevailing temper of a group or organisation is another important factor in developing leadership. Sticking to the analogy of the weather, it is plain what Montgomery meant by the 'atmosphere' in an organisation (p. 98). That kind of 'weather' is largely an invasion by the situation, or at least as people perceive it. When chill winds blow in the environment an organisation can catch a cold: it may even die of pneumonia. But organisational climate implies a longer-term ethos: the prevailing atmosphere generated *within* the organisation. In this sense we can imagine an organisation as a large market garden greenhouse. To some extent the people working inside can make their own climate.

There are many dials upon which the elements of climate, such as temperature and humidity, can be read. So it is with organisations. We want a warm, friendly atmosphere. That usually brings out the best in people, but it should not be cosy. To change the analogy, it is no good if the crew are snug down below drinking coffee and being friendly with each other if the ship is driving towards the rocks.

Clearly much of the ethos of an organisation will be set by its leaders. They need to articulate from time to time its guiding beliefs. It is they who will set an example of cheerfulness at all times, for difficult tasks do not preclude enjoyment and fun. They can demonstrate by example the importance of caring for individuals if you want them to care for the common enterprise in return. Are there distinctive elements in the character or tone of some organisations which encourage the spread of leadership at all levels? I believe there are. For outcomes of conditions that might be found in an organisational climate, see Fig. 14.3 below.

Leadership Development Factors in Organisational Climate	
Conditions	Notes
Centrifugal	Authority/power constantly tends to move from the centre (as opposed to a centripetal organisation, where it goes *to* the centre). Plenty of delegation is one symptom. Responsibility flows outwards.
Tolerance of mistakes	Without mistakes there is no progress. There is a policy of trust and confidence in people, backed by training.
Forward-looking	Despite past achievements a proud organisation is oriented towards the future. It thinks in terms of purpose, aims and objectives.
Teamwork	The emphasis falls upon working in teams and as one big team. Teams imply good leaders. Therefore they will be naturally encouraged to emerge.
More equality	Where most outward status distinctions are being progressively abandoned, people are perceived to be equal in value. Then leadership becomes that much more important for getting things done.

Fig. 14.3

The following short case-study of an organisation where none of these conditions are present will serve to underline the points.

Swinton Electrics made its name in the 1930s by manufacturing a range of really safe household electrical appliances, notably a range of fires. It grew to 5000 employees working on seven different sites. The son of the founder, who took over as Chairman and Managing Director in 1958, likes even middling decisions to be referred to him. Decisions flow up and vetoes come down. He sacked two general managers last year 'for exceeding their authority', although there are no job descriptions setting out such limits. 'One mistake and you are out', said one of them to me. No time or money or thought is being given to sponsoring innovation or tapping the creativity in the organisation. Yet imports from South Korea are now out-selling Swinton's modified 1930s range of appliances. Nobody talks about Swinton Electrics as a team 'more a one-man band, I should say', remarked one manager. 'If anything happened to the boss we should collapse. Not that we ever see his face around here'. There are rigid status barriers between grades of managers, as well as those which separate management from the work force. Recently the directors voted themselves a large salary increase, private health insurance scheme, extra pensions, school fees and rights to enormous severance pay – all at a time when the company's share of the market was falling rapidly. 'I don't mind the boss having a Jaguar', said one junior manager, 'or even a chauffeur, but does it have to be the most expensive Jaguar on the market with a cocktail cabinet fitted in it? There have been several cases of employees cheating on expense sheets. They were dismissed. But a director who 'borrowed' some labour to do up his own house has been kept on. A month ago the personnel manager of Swinton, a nephew of the founder, came to see me again. 'I have been thinking that we should be doing something', he began. 'Perhaps if you could run a few leadership training courses for our supervisors . . .'

What would you have said?

The climate or ethos of an organisation is primarily the responsibility of the senior leadership, for it cannot be divorced from the overall effectiveness of it in terms of achieving the common task, working as a team and developing individuals. Developing the leadership potential in individuals is a special instance of the third circle. Does the climate of the organisation hatch out leadership? Or does it stifle it?

10   The Chief Executive

'As the chief man of a city is, so will be the people', observed the author of Ecclesiastes. So much depends upon the top leader, not least in forming and implementing a strategy for developing leadership in the organisation. Indeed, as the entry by Jan Hildreth suggests, the new role of chief executive has evolved to meet the need for leadership at the top.

The emergence of the chief executive

History gives warning against the dangers of one man dominating a human organisation. The solitary leader can be most effective, but all too often power conflicts with responsibility. It is therefore unwise, if not impossible, for one man to manage alone.

A board of directors can ensure that power does not corrupt and that conflicts of interest are properly reconciled. A board can also provide the company with access to more advice and support than one man can provide.

The board needs to be a well-integrated team whose members all contribute to its effectiveness. Like any team, it needs a leader. This may be an independent chairman, a chairman who combines his role with that of chief executive, or an inner team of chairman and chief executive.

It is perfectly feasible for a board to appoint a general manager to run the company according to the rule book if initiative, judgement and quick reactions are not needed.

But growth in the size of companies and the development of modern trading methods have increasingly brought with them the need for quick adjustment in order to exploit the changes rarely absent from the business scene. Accordingly it has frequently become necessary to extend the powers of the general manager beyond those of supervision.

The general manager becomes the managing director with a seat on the board. And from there, those same pressures are likely to lead to the emergence of the chief executive.

If there is a distinction between the role of the managing director and the chief executive – and I believe there is – it is one of the degree of leadership required from each.

The managing director must run the show from his position as an equal among his fellow board members. The chief executive must lead both the board and the organisation; this includes running the people who are running the show.

In essence, the chief executive represents a fine compromise between the need of any human organization for a recognizable leader, and the needs of the parties interested in an enterprise for a committee to protect and balance their interests.

To succeed, or even to survive, in this most difficult of roles requires of the chief executive good health, humour, a resilience not given to many, and the powers of persuasion and personal leadership needed in both boardroom and workshop.

Jan Hildreth, former Director-General
of the Institute of Directors

The degree of leadership present in the chief executive soon becomes apparent when it comes to talking about the development of leadership within his organisation. There are three broad responses:

(a) Leadership is just what my managers need. Yes, go ahead and train them. Oh no, we do not need it in the boardroom – we are far too busy for that sort of thing.

(b) I see what you mean. But I am too old or set in my ways to change my ways. And that goes for my senior colleagues too. Yet we will give you all the support and backing we can. When are you running the first course? I'll come along.

(c) Leadership development? We are the ones who need it first. I'll arrange for my senior colleagues to form the first course. Then we shall take it from there. I see it very much as part of our strategy for this company over the next five years.

Even if the chief executive is committed himself – and leading by example, he still has to carry his top leadership team with him. That can be a formidable task. 'I have found,' said Lord Sieff, Chairman of Marks and Spencer, 'that management can be divided into three groups – those who pay lip service to the idea but do not care a damn about it, those who believe in it but do not know how to implement it, and the small number who believe in it and implement the policy of good human relations successfully. Most top management does not appreciate what such a policy implies, certainly not what a total commitment to it entails'.

The 1980s call for greater competence if not greatness in the leadership of chief executives, especially those at the head of the largest organisations – industrial, commercial and public service – in the land. In the last few years there are signs that such leaders are making their presence felt, although not enough of them. 'Some men are born great, some achieve greatness and some have greatness thrust upon them', wrote Francis Bacon.

The difference between great and ordinary leaders is rarely formal intellect but insight. The great man understands the essence of a problem – the ordinary leader grasps only the symptoms. The great man focuses on the relationship of events to each other – the ordinary leader sees only a series of seemingly disconnected events. The great man has a vision of the future which enables him to place obstacles into perspective: the ordinary leader turns pebbles in the road into boulders.

Henry Kissinger

But greatness should not be confused with the 'great man theory of history', that all we want is a great man to lead us and all will be well. Greatness in leadership today is much more a matter of teamwork: it is creating and leading a leadership team. One of its chief signs is the capacity to build up the leadership of subordinates by direct and indirect means.

SUMMARY

Few organisations are really geared to develop to the full the leadership potential within them. Sometimes this may be due to the fact that they place little or no premium upon it, assuming either that it is not important or that conventional management training will provide it. Other organisations may be ignorant of the full range of actions that have to be taken. The principles which determined organisation should apply are the same, but of course the ways in which they are applied will differ according to circumstances. Those principles are:

- Formulating a policy for leadership development at boardroom level

- Placing a priority on leadership potential in selection procedures

- Training leaders on properly-designed courses

- Planning careers so as to give appropriate experience

- Turning all line managers into leadership trainers 'on the job'

- Building a specialist resource in this area

- Evolving an organisational structure that favours the exercise of leadership

- Encouraging all leaders to 'own' their own self-development

- Securing a climate or ethos which supports good leadership

- Obtaining a positive lead from the top

CHECKLIST:
DOES YOUR ORGANISATION DEVELOP LEADERS?

	Yes	No

Do you have a clear strategy for building good human relations which includes developing leadership at every level? ☐ ☐

When selecting people for management jobs do you assess them in terms of their functional ability (task, team and individual) and the associated qualities of personality and character? ☐ ☐

Are appointed leaders given a minimum of two days of leadership training?

Always ☐ Sometimes ☐ Never ☐

Do you have some system for career development, so that future senior leaders broaden their experience and knowledge? ☐ ☐

Are all line managers convinced that they are the real leadership trainers, however effective they are in that role? ☐ ☐

Is there a specialist 'research and development' team who are keeping the organisation and its line managers up to date – and up to the mark? ☐ ☐

Has your organisational structure been evolved with good leadership in mind? ☐ ☐

Do leaders, actual or potential, realise that they are the ones who 'own' the problem of self-development? ☐ ☐

In the light of Figure 14.3 on p. 182 would you say that there was room for improving the organisational ethos?

A great deal ☐ Some ☐ None ☐

Are your top man and his key team really behind leadership development?

Whole-hearted ☐ Half-hearted ☐ Not yet ☐

15 Your Leadership Self-Development Programme

Leadership courses usually end with a session on *action points*. At this stage in the book – an individual course in leadership – you should be drawing together the various action points you have been writing down. They should form the basis for your leadership self-development programme. As all thinking forward has to be done in terms of priorities it may be helpful to divide your plan into

Short-term: points you can implement immediately, or within the next year

Middle-term: actions or developments that may take up to three years to complete

Long-term: states or stages you would like to achieve by some date in the 3–10 year range

Behind this approach lies the basic assumption of this book, namely, that you are the person who is primarily responsible for your own leadership development. Unless there is some leadership in you in the first place this book will not have spoken to you anyway. For, like Albert Schweitzer,

> I do not believe that we can put into anyone ideas which are not in him anyway. As a rule there are in everyone some good ideas, like tinder. But much of this tinder catches fire only when it meets some flame or spark from outside; that is, from some other person.

In tending that fire you can at best hope for a high degree of partnership with the organisation you happen to be working in at present. You have to see if it can come up with the right opportunities at the right time, for it can be frustrating to have the ability and not to be able to use it. You can teach a child all about the theory and principles of riding a bicycle, but there comes a day when you have to give him a bicycle to ride.

The key question, of course, is are you the right person for that job from the organisation's point of view as well as your own? Does your self-perception match up with the perceptions that others are forming of you? Are you ready for that opportunity?

Experience in successively more challenging or broader leadership positions is essential for those who are destined for senior leadership jobs. It should not be protracted. For, as Thomas Hardy said, 'experience is as to intensity and not duration'. But experience by itself, as we have seen, is only one pillar of learning. The other constitutes that growing body of theory, principles, ideas, examples, skills and techniques – your personal and practical leadership philosophy. One possible action point is to keep a notebook for further quotations, examples or ideas relevant to leadership as you come across them. You may also like to have a box file for articles or newspaper cuttings as well.

For leadership cannot really be taught, it can only be learnt. If you work hard at it – given a modicum of potential – you will improve. Indeed someone of modest natural ability who works hard at the task, team and individual circles will eventually outstrip a person of high natural ability who is lazy and instinctive about it, for the latter's faults will grow bigger like weeds over the years. He will not be able to transfer his learnings from one situation to another because he has never understood why he was successful in terms of principles. It is sad to see a natural leader go bad, but I have seen it happen more than once.

When a large oil company took on James Harrison they immediately put him on their 'high-flyer' list. In his case it was especially appropriate because he had been a jet fighter pilot in the Royal Air Force for ten years. Harrison bubbled over with self-confidence and talked much about his leadership. He was scornful of theory. 'I am good with people', he declared. 'Management is something I do naturally – flying by the seat of my pants, I call it'. As his career passed mid-point, he acquired a reputation for taking short cuts and for ruthlessness. He spent more and more time in the corridors of Head

Office seeking to intrigue his way forward. Baulked of the particular senior job he coveted, he lapsed into bitterness and cynicism, and eventually accepted early retirement.

Martin Jones joined about the same time as James Harrison and at first envied him his gifts. Conscious that he had less of a natural talent for leadership he worked hard at it. He attended courses, read books about leadership and talked to leaders. Gradually, without him being fully aware of the process, something of the essence of leadership began to rub off on him. He sought opportunities for practising leadership whenever they came his way. He broadened his knowledge of the business. Promotions followed. Then came a lucky break. James Harrison had been appointed to be managing director of the Australian subsidiary but refused to go – ostensibly for family reasons but subconsciously because he could not bear to leave the committees at Head Office. Moreover, he knew the Australian business was going downhill fast – a failure he did not want to be associated with. Martin Jones seized the chance. By his leadership he turned the Australian company into one of the most profitable parts of the group in an especially lean economic year. He was appointed to the main Board three years later. The Chairman, in his letter, referred to him as 'a born leader', which made Martin Jones smile.

That leads me to emphasise again one important way of improving your leadership in a fairly painless way. From our childhood at home and schooldays onwards we are all observing leaders. At work we have a first-hand experience of leadership at the receiving end. Alas, we so often forget in later life to do and be what we so much wanted our first boss to do and be.

EXERCISE 13

List three leaders that you have worked with
Rate them in order of good, adequate and weak
Now identify three characteristics which each had
From the nine characteristics choose two which have directly been responsible for changing your own approach

It is often easier to learn more about leadership from a bad leader rather than a good one, 'knowledge of good bought dear by knowing ill', as Shakespeare put it. It is a way of obeying the biblical precept of 'making the most of the time,

YOUR LEADERSHIP SELF-DEVELOPMENT PROGRAMME**

because the days are evil'. Good leadership is often so silent, so self-effacing that you are hardly aware of it, but bad leadership always shouts at you. You will see lack of awareness or understanding, insensitivity, want of firmness, missing functions, integrity over-compromised and a host of other shortcomings. Try to be objective, like a scientist, and observe the effects on the group and yourself in the three key areas. You may notice, in the words of Sir John Buckley, Chairman of Davey International, that 'there is almost no extreme of poor performance which cannot be reached by a person or a group of people given sufficient lack of encouragement'.

If you are fortunate you will work with leaders who exemplify some if not all of the principles in this book. If you are still more fortunate your leader will also be a mentor, a teacher. We get that word from an actual man named Mentor, the friend to whom Odysseus entrusted the education of his son Telemachus when he went off to the Trojan War. His name now signifies a wise counsellor or guide. Behind many managers there are such mentors in their early careers.

Andrew Carnegie owed much to his senior, Thomas A. Scott. As head of the Western Division of the Pennsylvania Railroad, Scott recognised talent and the desire to learn in the young telegrapher assigned to him. By giving Carnegie increasing responsibility and by providing him with the opportunity to learn through close personal observation, Scott added to Carnegie's self-confidence and sense of achievement. Because of his own personal strength and achievement, Scott did not fear Carnegie's aggressiveness. Rather, he gave it full play in encouraging Carnegie's initiative.

You could say that Carnegie was lucky to have such a boss. Luck, in the sense of events or circumstances which seem to work for you or against you, does certainly play a part in the career of any leader. If General Gott had not been killed in a plane crash, for instance, Montgomery would not have taken over the Eighth Army. You would be foolish if you did not recognise the hand of luck. It is an uncomfortable factor to live with, but it is undeniably there in every sphere of life. If you are going to be effective as a leader, however, you need to adopt a positive policy towards luck. The worst strat-

egy you can adopt is to rely upon luck, except in extreme
circumstances where there is literally nothing else you can do.
Much of modern management science is aimed at closing
down the area in which luck operates. Market research, for
example, is designed to take the element of uncertainty out
of making and selling goods. The same principle of closing
down the area of uncertainty can be applied to your career as
a leader. How do you do it? To some extent you can make
your own luck. 'A wise man will make more opportunities
than he finds', said Bacon. The story of engineer Michael
Moore on page 42 is an excellent example of that principle.
He could not find the opportunity to develop his own self-
sealing coupling in Plessey and so he started his own company.

Whether the opportunities come within your company or
elsewhere in your chosen field you will be an unlucky person
indeed if none come your way. If you set yourself firmly upon
the path of leadership you will begin to see such opportunities.

On being prepared

Occasionally, I have heard some young man say cynically that
advancement is usually the result of 'getting the lucky breaks.'
This is a defeatist attitude that I deplore. It would be less than
honest to say that good fortune – being there, in the right place,
when the lightning strikes – does not play its part. Yet when opportunity comes, even by chance, the man must be prepared, must
be able to deliver; otherwise, his triumph will be short-lived. A
steady rise to a position of pre-eminence most often comes with
hard work, constant effort at self-improvement – and devotion to
principle.

One day during my White House years, I called in an assistant –
a highly competent man of fine personality – and asked him if he
would like to have a more responsible and remunerative job
which was then open. I explained that he would be operating
rather independently, largely responsible for his own decisions.
He thought a moment and then said, 'No, I'd be no good at it. I am
a No. 2 man – and I think a good one – but I am not a No. 1 man. I
am not fitted for such a job, and I don't want it.

Although his answer startled me, I respected his honesty.
Moreover, this world always needs competent No. 2 men, also
good No. 3, No. 4 and No. 5 men – and each, on his own level,
can be a good performer.

Yet I would urge any young man with ambition never to be too
hasty in concluding that he doesn't have the stature for top
leadership. Often I have seen a man who had doubts about his
own resources rise to the occasion and perform with great competence when the opportunity finally came.[1]

Dwight D. Eisenhower

You may be given them 'out of the blue' or you may have to reach out and get them.

The more that you examine life (just as the more scientists study nature) the less the part that chance or luck seems to play in the world of your work if you are brutally honest with yourself. A woman spectator called out to a famous golfer during a tournament, 'Hey, that was a lucky shot!' The golfer turned round and said, 'Madame, the more I practise the luckier I get'. If you work hard at your trade – in this case leadership – you will attract opportunities like a magnet. The price is observing to the full, in every department of the art of leadership, the motto *Be prepared*. When they congratulated Louis Pasteur on his discovery, apparently by accident, he replied 'Chance favours only the prepared mind'. The secret therefore is to work hard at leadership today, and tomorrow will largely take care of itself. Seize the small opportunities, and the big ones will find their way to you.

How you will react in a very senior leadership position will not be known until you get there. You may drag it down to your own level of incompetence, or you may grow into the job. How you actually perform in that position will largely depend upon your self-development. As that progresses you may want to revise your preliminary estimate of how high a leadership mountain you can climb.

Keith studied mechanical engineering at University and went into the aircraft industry. After several years he found that his interest in people as well as machines led him naturally into management. The idea of leadership as the core of managing people was growing like a seed. As he said, 'orders are obtained by people, designs are carried out by people, products are made by machines operated by people, and plant is assembled and commissioned by people; in short, people are the most vital resource in the whole process of wealth generation'. At 35, after a training and self-development programme, he became head of the production department, the previous summit of his ambition. But Keith found he enjoyed senior leadership responsibility, and after much heart-searching accepted an even more responsible job as managing director of a subsidiary making aircraft parts in Canada. He now aims to be chief executive of a larger public company by his mid-40s.

Whether or not you are prepared to devote what Pasteur called 'patient studies and persevering efforts' to developing your leadership potential depends first upon your ability to stoke up the fires of a burning desire to succeed as a leader. Without that high degree of motivation you'll give up at the first signs of difficulty. That desire is partly a reflection of your level of ability. Mozart passionately wanted to write and play music because he had a genius for it. If leadership is your vocation you feel you *must* use and develop your gift for it, and you will be unhappy if you do not. But it is also in part a consequence of your commitment to a cause. 'Give me', said Oliver Cromwell, 'the russet-coated captain who knows what he is fighting for, and loves what he knows'. Your motivation to become a leader can be developed best by finding a sphere of work which you find absorbingly interesting and demandingly worthwhile. Then you will show infectious dedication to the job in hand.

Granted that you are reasonably well motivated to lead and have evolved a programme of self-development (which may involve the help of outside training agencies) in order to prepare yourself for the leadership opportunities awaiting you, there is one contingency that you need to think about in advance – failure. You will certainly encounter it in the exercise of leadership, for there can be no great success unless you are willing sometimes to work on the edge of failure. Using the three circles model and the rest of this book, work hard to diagnose, the *cause* of that failure. It may have lain within you, or in circumstances beyond your control. But you need to know. So you must ruthlessly track down the cause of failure as if you were investigating an aeroplane crash. You will not regain your confidence to fly again until you understand what went wrong and know that you have mended the fault in yourself or the organisation.

A man's success is made up of failures, because he experiments and ventures every day, and the more falls he gets, moves faster on . . . I have heard that in horsemanship he is not the good rider who never was thrown, but rather that a man will never be a good rider until he is thrown; then he will not be haunted any longer by the terror that he shall tumble, and will ride whither he is bound.   *Emerson*

Thus, failure can be your best teacher. It can also give you the priceless gift of humility. As the vice-president of an American company once said to me, 'I have had enough success to keep me from despair, and enough failure to keep me humble'.

The essential elements in leadership self-development are

1 knowing the principles
2 plenty of practice
3 learning from feedback

Leadership is fun

My obligation as a manager is to manage in a way that enables the needs of the business to be met and the joint objectives of my colleagues and myself to be achieved. In bringing this about I have the responsibility to see that the people responsible to me who are fulfilling the task have the opportunity to extract satisfaction and fun in doing it. Yes, I do mean fun. Difficult tasks do not preclude enjoyment and fun; when the fun goes out of a job one should seriously consider whether one is equipped to cope – being a manager today certainly requires a sense of humour.

The occasions on which I have gained most personal satisfaction from heading up a team have been when the going has been really tough and yet one is conscious of the enormous support and enthusiasm from that team of people. I believe, however, that the effort which has to be made by every member of the team in order to achieve that unity of purpose is far greater than any demands which the task in itself could present. It is also far more rewarding. If we try to evaluate that effort against the demands of the task it is like trying to judge whether we would have recovered from pneumonia if we had not taken the unpleasant drugs. We will never know but we are thankful to be still alive. Creating a working environment which gives satisfaction to those operating in it is an objective in itself. This does not imply it should be an easy environment but it should be a rewarding one in terms of job satisfaction.

It does not require a genius to spell out that you need to manufacture wealth before you can distribute it but it is not always understood by those outside manufacturing industry that it is not even this indisputable fact that drives so many managers to want to contribute to the success of their company and who could deny that a successful company must first be a profitable one. It is the mixture of enthusiasm, striving to achieve a goal, maximising resources and enthusing others which adds to the appeal of the successful leader.

A definition which I probably share with many other managers is what true leadership is not about – it is not about power; it is about a person's legitimate right to lead through example and self discipline. Most of us, at least, recognise it, admire it, and respond when we see it displayed.[2]

Ann Mansell

The essential point made by Ann Mansell in the above quotation is that leadership should be seen as enjoyable and rewarding. If you begin to see it in that light you will want to become better at it.

When it comes to developing your burning desire, remember that *imagination* is the leader of *willpower*. Schoolboys day-dream of becoming famous: they visualise themselves as carrying out some heroic exploit or making a great discovery. Purposeful day-dreaming is how nature prepares us for the future. If you want to increase your motivation start by using your imagination. Picture where you want to be and how you want to behave. Don't give up because you feel you lack sufficient motivation at the moment. Within limits you can do something about that, especially as you come to know better what triggers off your own energy most effectively.

EXERCISE 14

Are you confident that you have chosen the right field of work in which to exercise leadership?

How would you rate your motivation or desire to improve your own leadership ability?

> burning fiercely ....
> warm flame ....
> glowing embers ....
> fire seems out ....

Can you already imagine yourself in a senior leader position?

Somebody once called golf 'the humbling game'. How much more so is the exercise of leadership! Here you are competing essentially against yourself. If you feed upon your strengths and starve your weaknesses, if you apply the principles of leadership, your performance as a leader will certainly get better, but there is always more waiting to be learned. Once you get to one level, you will espy the next ridge of quality ahead. You may feel, for example, that you have mastered the functions of planning, controlling and appraising. But is that the whole of leadership? Another crest looms up ahead, it is the ability to inspire. And so it will go on. For leadership attracts us because it is such an inexhaustible subject. As you go deeper into it you see that skill and technique are not enough by themselves.

> Efficiency of a practical flawless kind may be achieved naturally in the struggle for bread. But there is something beyond – a higher point, a subtle and unmistakable touch of love and pride beyond mere skill; almost an inspiration which gives to all work that finish which is almost art – which *is* art.
>
> *Joseph Conrad*

If this book has succeeded, it should have given you at least some glimpses of what that 'subtle and unmistakable touch of love' means within the context of leadership.

The prayer of a famous leader

Lord, make me an instrument of your peace!
  Where there is hatred, let me sow love,
  Where there is injury, pardon;
  Where there is doubt, faith;
  Where there is despair, hope;
  Where there is darkness, light;
  Where there is sadness, joy.
O Divine Master, grant that I may not so much seek
  to be consoled, as to console;
  to be understood, as to understand;
  to be loved, as to love.
For it is in giving that we receive;
It is in pardoning that we are pardoned;
It is in dying that we are born to eternal life.

Francis of Assisi

EXERCISE 15
OPERATION SELF-DEVELOPMENT

Choose three objectives from the following list to incorporate in your *leadership self-development programme* over the next five years:

1 To participate in at least two short courses in the field of 'the human side of enterprise', such as public-speaking, communication, leadership, interviewing skills or decision making and creative thinking.
2 To interview formally or informally five proven leaders you

respect in order to listen to their ideas on leadership and to learn how they came by them. Not more than three of these leaders should be in your own industry or profession.

3 To ask ten people not in your working group or organisation what they value most in their leader's behaviour – and what they value least. Record the answers in your notebook.

4 To read one thought provoking or stimulating book about leadership or the management of people in each of the five years, recording a minimum of five action points from each.

5 To answer within the next three months the following questions:

    (i) What are my personal objectives in my working life?

    (ii) What purpose in my life do they serve?

    (iii) What value do I place on attaining those objectives?

    (iv) When are they going to be accomplished? What is my programme?

    (v) Where do I stand now? Where am I going from here?

    (vi) How can I improve my present performance?

    (vii) Who are my most helpful advisers and critics?

6 To get accurate assessments of what the organisation you work for thinks about your leadership potential. To find out and appraise the organisation's programme for developing your potential in this period. (Warning: it may require more moral courage than you possess at present to tackle your boss on this errand!)

7 To evolve a contingency plan in case your organisation does not give you a real opportunity to exercise more leadership in the next five years.

8 If your present job does not give you much chance to develop leadership, or if it does not use all your abilities, choose another field (youth services, community, local government, church, politics) in which you can add to your track-record of leadership. The change of situation should stretch you and stimulate you.

9 Offer to carry out in your own spare time and without charge a leadership survey of a local organisation e.g. a charity or service which is not doing very well. Use the three-circles model to diagnose what is wrong. Come up with an action programme – including a leadership training course and implement it.

10 'Authority flows from the man who knows'. Select one

long course (not less than four weeks – not more than three months) which is going to enhance or widen your knowledge of management in general – finance, marketing, production, distribution and personnel. Work out a plan for persuading your company that it is in their interests to send you on it.

Which three objectives have you chosen?

Objective no.   Completion date

_____   _____
_____   _____
_____   _____

CONCLUSION

Your *leadership self-development programme* should reflect your commitment and burning desire to make the most of your talents. It should focus as much as possible on practical steps. For if you do the right things you will become a leader. There is no magic about it, nor is there any recipe for instant success. Do not wait for the right attitudes to appear – that can take years. Actions form attitudes. If you form a picture of the person you would like to be – drawing upon models or examples of real leaders – then all things will begin to work together to grow into that stature. Experience and theory, success and failure, friend and foe, will all help you in one way or another. Do not be afraid of taking bold initiatives, even risks, with your career especially if you are aiming high. The good news is that there is always more about leadership to be learned. No one person knows it all or does it all. What matters most is that you are now moving steadily higher on the path of leadership, setting past failures or disappointments firmly behind you. For the true leader, like Wordsworth's 'Happy Warrior'

> Looks forward, persevering to the last,
> From well to better, daily self-surpast.

CHECKLIST:
YOUR LEADERSHIP SELF-DEVELOPMENT PROGRAMME

	Yes	No
Have you now drafted a programme of action or growth points which covers the		
Short-term (tomorrow – 12 months)	☐	☐
Middle-term (1–3 years)	☐	☐
Long-term (4–10 years)	☐	☐
Have you entered into your diary some dates for progress reviews?	☐	☐
Can you discuss your plans with anyone at work or outside it to establish if they are		
too ambitious	☐	☐
too modest	☐	☐
too vague	☐	☐
too unrealistic	☐	☐

What would you say has been the key sentence in this book as far as you are concerned? Write it here:

	Yes	No
Are you prepared to read that sentence again in six months' time to see if it has had any effect on your leadership?	☐	☐
Have you identified three objectives from the list of ten in 'Operation Self-Development' and incorporated them in your programme?	☐	☐
Now turn back to that exercise (p. 197) and choose three more for consideration in one year's time – if not already covered in your programme. Can you do that?	☐	☐

Appendix 1
Answers to Exercises

EXERCISE 1 (pages 12–13)

Ranking of attributes rated most valuable at top level of management by a cross-section of successful chief executives.

1 Ability to take decisions
2 Leadership
3 Integrity
4 Enthusiasm
5 Imagination
6 Willingness to work hard
7 Analytical ability
8 Understanding of others
9 Ability to spot opportunities
10 Ability to meet unpleasant situations
11 Ability to adapt quickly to change
12 Willingness to take risks
13 Enterprise
14 Capacity to speak lucidly
15 Astuteness
16 Ability to administer efficiently
17 Open-mindedness
18 Ability to "stick to it"
19 Willingness to work long hours
20 Ambition
21 Single-mindedness
22 Capacity for lucid writing
23 Curiosity
24 Skill with numbers
25 Capacity for abstract thought

EXERCISE 2 (pages 17–20)

1 Companies with rapid growth and problems of change, with high or advanced technology and relatively small in size.
2 (1) A worthwhile and safe product.
 (2) Encourage a learning staff, one eager to acquire new knowledge and skills.
 (3) Consult and involve people by clear and honest communication.

(4) Appoint leaders who are optimistic, cheerful and enthusiastic.

(5) Build a positive climate or style, one which encourages managers to give their best.

3. No? Neither did I at first. But if you think about it again when you have finished this book, you may see that the principles *can* be applied in any organisation, although in other ways or differing degrees. So do not close your mind too early on this question.

EXERCISE 3 (page 23)

Donald Seaman continues:

> I said to the rebel soldier who had asked for my opinion: "Anyone can seize command in a war. But to know when to show mercy is the test of *leadership*."
>
> The members of the court martial let the boy grovel while they talked it over among themselves. For 20 minutes he knelt in front of them, sobs shaking his body.
>
> Then they said to me: "Well, it might look bad if we shot him in front of you."
>
> So they spared him, though for how long I do not know because it was time for me to move on out of that sector.
>
> *Daily Express*, 15 April 1971

EXERCISE 6 (pages 56–7)

More Leadership Characteristics		
Quality	Useful	Not Useful
Efficiency	Especially in task area, as measured by a constant comparison of work done with its cost in energy, time and money. Relevant to team work and self-management as well.	When carried to extremes, ignoring the human factor. When it becomes an end in itself, divorced from effectiveness.
Industry	When it means intelligent or clever working as well as diligence or hard-working in any task. Steady application pays dividends.	As over-work, leading to excessive tiredness and tension. The 'workaholic' loses confidence in subordinates, procrastinates in

(continued)

Quality	Useful	Not Useful
		decision making, fails to delegate properly and becomes unnecessarily involved in minutiae.
Audacity	When its bold disregard of restraints of convention or prudence works. If it comes across as intrepid daring, originality and verve. Can be applied to team and individual areas, as well as task.	Audacity as contempt of custom or decorum. Insolence or impudence can destroy human relations. When it becomes just gambling, i.e. not taking a numerate and logical approach to decision making.
Honesty	Always wins respect of group and each individual. As adherence to facts, it helps in the task area.	When 'white lies' are called for e.g. 'all brides are beautiful'. Candour or frankness at wrong times or in wrong places.
Self-confidence	If you do not trust yourself and your powers, why should others? Therefore essential for leaders.	When it degenerates into self-conceit – an exaggerated opinion of one's qualities or abilities.
Justice	The principle of just or fair dealing, e.g. in adjusting conflicting claims, sharing rewards or disciplining, is vital for team-building.	In situations that call for creative love rather than strict or exact justice.
Moral courage	Required in situations of danger, fear or difficulty or when you have to tell the truth, or when you have to stand up for right conduct.	When it is in such short supply that your anxiety becomes contagious, or you compromise on a principle, or you cannot face a subordinate.
Consistency	Lack of contradictions in your behaviour creates a feeling of security and 'knowing where we stand'.	When you become too predictable. When it is confused with inflexibility.

EXERCISE 7 (pages 63–4)

A national newspaper invited its readers to submit solutions. The following was considered the simplest:

1 Lay poles D across G–J, slightly apart and under triangle F;
2. Edge drum C along poles D until it is centrally under diagonal H;
3. Group walk on poles D, step onto near end of drum C, step through triangle F back onto far end of drum C and walk on poles D to J;
4. When all across recover drum C and poles D.

The leader must   a) Brief his team on the method
                       illustrated below
                   b) Select the four heaviest to go through first
                   c) Choose the pair strongest to lift the drum onto poles
                   d) Choose the lightest (last man through)
                       in advance, before starting.

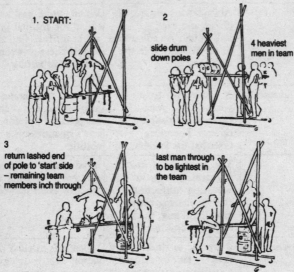

– after last man through, withdraw poles. END

Having used this exercise with civil engineering students at the University of Surrey another solution has emerged:

1 Position poles and oil drum
2 Step up into drum. Walk through gap F back on to drum and step off
3 Remove drum and poles from opposite side.

Comments on the group

As you probably guessed, it was difficult to prevent Henry from taking over the group, but he had some experience of these kinds of exercises on Scouting courses, which was useful to you. Simon kept coming up with complicated engineering plans, as if he was building a bridge over a motorway. Sally talked so much you had to ask her to keep quiet twice when she was interrupting, but she did have the germ of the idea which led to your solution. Jim showed lots of initiative and enthusiasm. Despite the rain he kept at it doing the jobs you gave him with considerable agility. The group were pleased when the agreed solution worked, but they are still wondering if they considered *all* the feasible options and chose the simplest one. What do you think now?

EXERCISE 9 (pages 88–9)

1 Many people unconsciously place a framework around the dots. They are making an assumption without realising it. But the problem can only be solved by going outside those invisible, self-imposed barriers, thus:

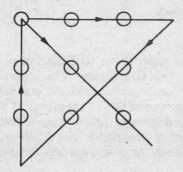

2 With the six matchsticks, too, people try to solve the problem in two dimensions. The most elegant solution, however, is to break that assumption and build a three-dimensional pyramid. A 'Star of David' arrangement is also acceptable. It involves some creativity, because you are at least putting matchsticks on top of each other, but it is less exciting.

Appendix 2
Analysis of a
Leadership Situation

The following text, a brief description of a British expedition
to Greenland in 1930, is used to illustrate the functional approach to the study of leadership and the method by which
a leadership situation may be analysed to determine the needs
existing within the group and thus what may be required of
the leader.

The leader of the expedition, Gino Watkins, was most
successful in his role but his leadership is not being offered
as an example for unthinking emulation. It was suitable for
this leader, with his particular group which was working in
an unusual situation.

GINO WATKINS

Gino Watkins led expeditions to Edge Island (near Spitzber-
gen), Labrador and Greenland. This extract from J. M.
Scott's biography concerns his leadership in Greenland during
1930. The average age of the 14 members of the party was 25
years old, eighteen months more than Watkins. He died in
1933, drowned in a Greenland lake while out hunting in a
kayak. Posthumously he was awarded the Polar Medal with
Arctic clasp.

> As quietly as if it had been a Scottish shooting-party Gino
> had organised the greatest British expedition to the Arctic for
> half a century, and he was carrying it through in the same
> unofficial, unheroic spirit . . . When he sailed for Edge Island
> he had no first-hand knowledge of the conditions. He was
> successful because he could sum up positions quickly and act
> without hesitation, and he was a tactful and popular leader
> because he asked the opinions of the members of the party
> who had each some special knowledge to impart. In Labrador

it had been the same. Everyone he came in contact with was gratified by his respectful interest in all they said and, without fully realising it, they did what he wanted them to do and taught him all the useful knowledge they possessed. In England he had read widely and had asked pertinent questions whenever he met well-travelled men, so that by now he knew a great deal about polar technique; and although he was no scientist he understood clearly enough what the specialists were after . . .

He did what he enjoyed and visited the places that he wanted to visit, but, being there, he used all the resources in his power to bring back everything he could. By knowledge he was best qualified to lead to Greenland quite apart from the fact that he had created the expedition. Most of the party had seen little of him before they sailed, and they were ready to treat him at least with the outward deference they were accustomed to show to a commander. If he had enjoyed that sort of thing he could very easily have kept it up. But his sense of humour made it absurd. He took trouble to climb down from this uncomfortable eminence by telling stories against himself, flirting with the Eskimos, posing as an utter Philistine or joining in every menial task . . .

Besides, he gave himself no privileges at all. His bed was no more comfortable than ours; probably it was less so, judging by the dog harness and rifles which were piled on top of it. His clothes were no better and his private possessions far less numerous. His dogs I had given to him after selecting what I considered the best team for myself. Only his native hunting instruments were superior because he had taken great trouble in acquiring them. I was reminded that once in Labrador I heard a man call him Boss, and Gino had been a little embarrassed and very much amused. That was not his name, so why address him so?

As unemotionally as one is conscious of a fact of life, he knew that he would lead in any circumstance. Neither familiarity nor conventional discipline could alter that, and he preferred familiarity because he had no wish to be lonely. He was a young man who set out to enjoy himself and to make others enjoy themselves as well, because he believed that people work better when they are happy.

All that was comparatively easy. Almost anybody with a sense of humour could have done as much if his sole object was to be accepted as a member of the party. But to one who was responsible for making people do unpleasant tasks it was a self-imposed handicap which could only be overcome by a very high type of personality. There could be no bluffing in such leadership, it would either prove magnetic by its inspiring originality or lead to chaos by its non-existence.

At first there was some argument as to Gino's wisdom in following the course which he had chosen. People like the Bedouin are used to such methods: they expect a leader to be one of themselves and recognise a strong character most easily in contrast to circumstances which they themselves experience . . . One or two of the Service men in particular were upset by the apparently casual suggestions which passed for commands. Gino said it was absurd to write to a man you could talk to; but even so, they would have appreciated the comfortable definiteness of written orders, if only to assure them that they had done all that was expected. Others, although they could not have admitted it, had looked for something more in exploration: a consciousness of adventure and romance. All this was so straightforward and matter-of-fact that if one so much as grew a beard one felt theatrical. Gino's plans and his rebellious why-not? points of view were exciting enough if one could swallow them; but without experience we had no personal standard to judge by; and could anyone so casual have taken trouble to prepare the best equipment?

As time passed and experience brought knowledge, these doubts were laid one after another. It very soon became apparent that the equipment was extraordinarily good. The clothing was light and warm, while the sledging rations – Gino's most striking innovation – were excellent; no one had been really hungry on any journey and there had only been one serious case of frostbite. The sledging tents, lighter and easier to pitch than the older Antarctic models, had withstood considerable storms. The dome-shaped tent at the ice-cap station, which was designed somewhat on the lines of an Eskimo igloo with a tunnel entrance and small tube ventilator at the apex, had so far proved efficient, though it had not yet had to withstand the hardest test of all. The Base hut, with its double walls and central kitchen, was warm and well designed. These facts and a thousand little things bore proof of care and foresight.

The work of the first season proved remarkably successful. Luck played a part, as in the absence of heavy ice at Kangerdlugsuak, but luck is a valuable addition to a leader's reputation. In detail the journeys had not developed exactly as expected; but the acting leaders, unrestricted by precise directions yet understanding very clearly the general objective, had used their initiative to achieve a useful end. In the course of our work we had done things that we had never done before – we had driven dogs and navigated small boats through ice – and we had found these things remarkably easy. Knowing that so much had depended upon ourselves, our self-confidence increased and with it our confidence in Gino; for his plans were only alarming when we doubted our ability to fulfil our part in them. Having discovered the surprising fact that we were as good men as Gino thought we were, we accepted him as a splendid leader. He was exacting, he was ruthlessly indifferent to small discomforts like cold or unvaried fresh meat diets at the Base, he was disconcerting in his words and actions, but he would never be at a loss and would never blame. Once only Gino remarked that a man was beginning to behave badly and that he thought he would have to have a row with him. He had his row, in a roaring temper, so it seemed, and afterwards they were far stronger friends than they had been before.

If he told inexperienced men to do what they thought best, and if they made some fatal blunder, the responsibility would be his just as surely as if he had expressly ordered that disastrous action. The world would see it thus and so would he. It was a risky policy, but for his purpose the risk was unavoidable.

Briefly, his method of leadership was to train each man to be a leader: his ideal exploring party consisted of nothing else. These were young men and he was looking ahead towards other, more perplexing, quests.

In Gino's opinion, initiative and self-confidence were all-important and so he would keep nobody in leading-strings. The boy who stood on the burning deck seemed to him nothing but a fool. Once, too, he had gone to a film about the sinking of a great liner. When he saw the last brave men, who had put the women and children in the only boats, standing at attention to sing, 'Nearer, my God, to Thee', he turned to his neighbour in the darkness and in an urgent whisper said, 'Why the hell don't they build rafts instead of wasting their time being heroic?' From the same coldly practical point of view he had told me on our last journey that if the food ran out and he himself should die he would naturally expect to be eaten; and, when I demurred, he added, 'Well, I'd eat you, but then, of course, you are much more fat and appetising . . .'

He did not preach this philosophy which I have attempted to explain. He followed the path which he had chosen, enjoying every step, quick to shock, slow to offend, but caring nothing how his words and actions were interpreted when he felt their aim was right, leading without looking back because he knew that we would follow him. Both as a friend and a leader he had always something in reserve, some depth which gave occasional proof of its existence, but which even he did not understand. The one aspect aroused interest and the other confidence.

ANALYSIS

This total situation can be broken down into its components and analysed as follows:

Elements of the Working Situation	Needs	Leadership Functions
1. The Leader a. Younger than the group but possessed greater knowledge and experience of the Arctic.	**1. Group Needs** a. Being newly formed, lacked group identity, knowledge of, or faith in, the leader and each other.	**1. Group Functions** a. Didn't seek privileges or abuse his position as leader and founder of the expedition.
b. Not a scientist but he understood what the specialists were after.	b. Discipline and team work essential.	b. Set out to make others enjoy themselves because he believed that people work better when they are doing so.
c. A self-appointed leader.	c. Group's approach had to be practical, down to earth – not romanticised.	c. He led by example.
d. Confident in his role as leader.		d. Maintained discipline – had his row but retained the punished man as an accepted member of the group.
e. A sense of humour and humility		e. Exacting but fair to his men.

Elements of the Working Situation	Needs	Leadership Functions
f. A rather unique, inspiring personality. g. By nature an easy going, democratic, 'participative' type of leader.		f. Developed confidence of the team in himself and in each other.
2. The Group a. All volunteers and thus well motivated.	2. Individual Needs a. Food, dress and equipment suitable for the harsh environment.	2. Individual Functions a. Provided top quality equipment – clothing, tents, sledge, rations.
b. Some servicemen, used to direct and specific orders, the remainder mainly scientists.	b. Physical security, ie. survival.	b. Trained team members in basic skills in such a way as to develop self-confidence and initiative.
c. Little or no experience in Arctic conditions.	c. Training in 'local' skills.	
d. Little or no skill in Arctic techniques.	d. Development of self-reliance, self-confidence and initiative.	
3. The Situation a. Task: exploration and various scientific experiments and projects.	3. Task Needs a. Careful planning, preparation and launching of the expedition.	3. Task Functions a. He clearly defined general objectives but refrained from precise, restricting orders so that sub-leaders could react to unforeseeable circumstances.

Elements of the Working Situation	Needs	Leadership Functions
b. Small groups to work away from the main party for varying periods. c. A hostile environment involving personal danger and requiring special techniques for living, working and movement.	b. Clear definition of tasks but freedom of action by small groups in the execution.	b. He adopted a style of leadership which: (1) Suited his personality (a lesser personality could not have adopted such an unconventional approach). (2) Suited the situation – an authoritarian approach would have restricted the growth of confidence/initiative and would not have allowed the flexibility necessary in groups working away from the leader.

CONCLUSION

The above analysis lists the various factors, needs and functions under convenient group headings. Obviously, many of the points cannot be isolated completely in this way. As discussed in Chapter 3, the total situation is the result of the interaction of the leader, the group and the situation within which they are working. A function performed by the leader to satisfy a need in one area may well have an effect for good or ill in some other area.

A good example of this is the effect achieved by the care and foresight used by Watkins in the preparation and selection of equipment. Not only did he provide for the phsyical needs of his men, but the confidence developed by the group in his ability as a leader was a significant factor in welding the newly formed group into an effective team.

References

Chapter 1: What you have to be

1 G. W. Allport and H. A. Odbert, 'Trait-names: A Psychological Study', *Psychological Monographs*, No. 211, 1936.
2 C. Bird, *Social Psychology*, Appleton-Century, 1940.
3 C. A. Gibb (ed), *Leadership: Selected Readings*, Penguin, 1969. Contains a reprint of R. M. Stogdill's article.

Chapter 2: What you have to know

1 W. O. Jenkins, 'A Review of Leadership Studies with Particular Reference to Military Problems', *Psychological Bulletin*, vol. 44, 1947.
2 'Leadership in the Elga Group', *The Industrial Society*, December 1980.
3 Peter Young, *Bedouin Command* and *Storm from the Sea*, William Kimber, 1956 and 1958, both convey the flavour of this natural military leader.

Chapter 3: What you have to do

1 G. Whitaker, *T-Group Training: Group Dynamics in Management Education*, Association of Teachers of Management, Occasional Papers 2, Blackwell, 1965.
   D. Cartwright and A. Zander, *Group Dynamics: Research and Theory*, Tavistock, 1960.
2 R. R. Blake and Jane Mouton, *The Managerial Grid*, Gulf Publishing Co., 1967.
3 F. E. Fiedler, *A Theory of Leadership Effectiveness*, McGraw-Hill, 1967.
4 John W. Hunt, *Managing People at Work*, Pan, 1981 (Chapter 7); Dian-Marie Hosking, 'A Critical Evaluation of Fiedler's Contingency Hypothesis', *Progress in*

Applied Social Psychology, ed. G. M. Stephenson and J. M. Davis, John Wiley, 1981.

5 Paul Hersey and Kenneth H. Blanchard, *Management of Organisational Behaviour: Utilising Human Resources*, 3rd edition, Prentice-Hall, 1977.

6 March-April, 1958.

7 F. A. Heller, *Managerial Decision-Making: A Study of Leadership Styles and Power Sharing*, Tavistock, 1971.

8 Gallup Poll on European Attitudes, 1981.

9 A. H. Maslow, *Motivation and Personality*, Harper, 1954.

10 W. G. Bennis and E. H. Schein (ed), *Essays of Douglas McGregor*, M.I.T. Press, 1966.

Chapter 4: Pulling the threads together

1 G. Lindzey and E. Aronson (ed), *Handbook of Social Psychology*, vol. 2, Addison-Wesley, 1954.

2 M. Taylor, *Coverdale on Management*, Heinemann, 1979.

3 A. H. Maslow, *Eupsychian Management: A Journal*, Richard D. Irwin, 1965.

4 H. Fayol, *General and Industrial Management*, Pitman, 1949.

5 Chester Barnard, *The Functions of the Executive*, Harvard, 1938.

6 Lyndall F. Urwick, *Elements of Administration*, Harper, 1944.

7 R. Tannenbaum and W. H. Schmidt, 'How to choose a leadership pattern – Retrospective Commentary', *Harvard Business Review*, May-June 1973.

8 A portrait of John Lord is contained in *To Revel in God's Sunshine: the Story of Academy Sergeant Major J. C. Lord*, MVO, MVE, compiled by R. Alford, privately printed, 1977.

9 'The Eisenhower Story', *National Geographic*, July 1969.

10 N. Heap, 'Training in the 80's', *Industrial Society*, June 1981

Chapter 5: Some practical applications

1 H. Harris, *The Group Approach to Leadership Testing*, Routledge and Kegan Paul, 1949.

2 See also *Leadership Training: A Report on the Application of Action-Centred Leadership*, The Industrial Society, 1970 (available in British Institute of Management Library).

Chapter 7: Planning

1 For a good short guide, see Julia Morland, *Quality Circles*, The Industrial Society, 1981. The author discusses the advantages of Quality Circles under the headings of Task, Team and Individual.

Chapter 8: Briefing

1 N. Hamilton, *Monty: The Making of a General*, Hamish Hamilton, 1981.
2 H. C. Metcalf and L. Urwick, *Dynamic Administration: The Collected Papers of Mary Parker Follett*, Harper, 1940. See also Asa Briggs, *Social Thought and Social Action: A Study of the Work of Seebohm Rowntree*, Longmans, 1951.

See also: Ian McDougall, *A Guide to Team Briefing*, The Industrial Society, 1981. This short booklet describes the systematic approach to communication which The Industrial Society has advocated for some twenty years.

Chapter 10: Evaluating

1 L. Russell, 'A Re-Appraisal on Formal Performance Appraisal Interviewing', *Training*, November 1978.

Chapter 11: Motivating

1 Douglas McGregor, *The Human Side of Enterprise*, McGraw-Hill, 1961.
2 J. Sterling Livingston, 'Pygmalion in Management', *Harvard Business Review*, July/Aug., 1969, vol. 47, No. 4, p. 81.
3 F. Herzberg et al., *The Motivation to Work*, Wiley, 1959, and *Work and the Nature of Man*, World Publishing Co., 1966.

Chapter 12: Organising

1 J. A. C. Brown, *The Social Psychology of Industry*, Penguin, 1954.
2 P. G. Gyllenhammar, *People at Work*, Addison-Wesley, 1977.
3 Montgomery, *The Path to Leadership* Collins, 1961.
4 P. Drucker, *The Effective Executive*, Heinemann, 1967.

Chapter 13: Setting an example

1 R. Baker, *Dry Ginger: The Biography of Admiral of the Fleet Sir Michael Le Fanu*, W. H. Allen, 1979.
2 'Make way for unity', *Industrial Society*, July/August 1979. See also: P. Prior, *Leadership is not a Bowler Hat*, David and Charles, 1977.

Chapter 14: Does your organisation develop leaders?

1 From an unpublished lecture given at St. George's House, Windsor, entitled 'Leadership – An Historical Perspective', 1979.
2 David Stinton, *Air Clues*, (Royal Air Force Journal), November 1968.
3 C. Margerison, 'How Chief Executives Succeed', *Journal of European Training*, vol. 4, no. 5, 1980.
4 Chester Barnard, *The Functions of the Executive*, Harvard, 1938.

Chapter 15: Your leadership self-development programme

1 'Eisenhower, The Art of Leadership', *Reader's Digest*, July 1965.
2 A. Mansell, 'Leadership is fun', *Industrial Society*, January/February 1979.

Index

Ability, natural, 189–90, 194
Absence agreements, 72
Accountability, 44
Achievement as motivation, 133
Action plans, 121, 122
Action-Centred Leadership (ACL)
   courses, 67–74, 93, 169, 174–5
Advancement as motivation, 137
Aesthetic needs, 37
Aims, 78, 79, 80, 81
Alexander the Great, 79
Alternatives, searching for, 84–7
America, 31–3, 34
American Civil War, 111
Analysis of a leadership situation,
   206–12
Anxiety, 110
Application, 66
Appointed leaders, 44, 85
Appointments, personnel, 124
Appraisal interviews, 119–24, 178
   guidelines for, 120–1
   questions in, 123–4
Arctic expeditions, 206–10
Aristotle, 55, 79
Assertiveness, 94, 105
Assumptions, 87–8, 116
   about man, 130
Attitudes to leadership
   development, 185
Attlee, Clement, 27, 108, 115
Audacity, 203
Australian Army, 68
Authority, 16, 45, 85–6, 105
Authority-freedom continuum,
   52–3

Awareness of leadership, 1

Bad temper, 109–10
Bacon, Francis, 165, 192
Bangladesh rebels, 23
Barnard, Chester, 51
Barnett, Corelli, 170
Behaviourism, 31, 58
Bennis, W.G., 45
Bird, Professor C., 8
Bismarck, Otto von, 88
Blake, R.R., 31
Blanchard, K.H., 32
Bonnington, Chris, 86, 160
Bonus schemes, 71–2
Bradley, General, 59
Brainstorming 89–90, 166
Brearley, Mike, 34–5
Briefing, 93–104
   for groups, 94–9
   for individuals, 102
   for organisations, 100–2
Briefing groups, 73, 100
Briefing skills, 95
British Steel, 99–100
Brooke, Sir Alan, 59
Buchan, John, 140
Buckley, Sir John, 191
Bureaucracy, 101
Butler, Samuel, 54

Cabinet, 27, 108, 115
Calmness in action, 111
Career development policy, 175–7
Career profile, 175, 177
Carnegie, Andrew, 119, 191

Casualness, 208
Chalfont, Lord, 19
Character, 10–11
Checklists
 briefing, 104
 company leadership, 69
 controlling, 113
 defining the task, 82
 developing leaders, 187
 evaluating, 127–8
 leadership qualities, 14
 leadership self-development
  programme, 200
 motivating, 141
 organising, 158
 planning one's work, 92
 setting an example, 166
 situational change, 25
 three circles, 48
Chief executives, 183–6
Churchill, Sir Winston, 17, 56,
 57, 59, 87, 111, 124
Cicero, 124
Climate
 group, 89
 organisational, 181–3
Coggan, Dr. Donald, 147–8
Cognitive needs, 37
Cohesiveness, group, 63
Command, quality of, 65
Communication
 non-verbal, 30, 108, 165
 of objectives, 77–8, 79–81
 skills, 94, 123
 systems, 143
Compassion, 55, 111
Confidence, 67, 203, 209
Conrad, Joseph, 197
Consensus testing, 30, 86, 108
Consequences, assessing, 114–17
Consistency, 53, 203
Consultation of employees,
 18–19, 74, 116
Contingency plans, 90–1
Contingency theory of leadership
 effectiveness, 32
Control systems, 108–9
Controlling, 105–13
 meetings, 107–8
 organisations, 108–9
 self-control, 109–11

Coolness, 65–6
Courage, moral, 32, 203
Courses, leadership, 178; see also
 Action-Centred Leadership
 courses
Courtesy, 102
Creative thinking, 42, 87–8, 172–3
Credit for achievements, 133
Cricket, 34–5
Crisis situations, 21, 22–3, 52
Criticism, 89, 120
Cromwell, Oliver, 124, 194

De-briefing, 117–18
Decision making, 51–4, 84–7, 143
 styles of, 53–4
Defining the task, 77–82
De Guingand, Brigadier, 99
Delegation, 136–7, 148,
 152–4, 208–9
 delegation v. abdication, 152
Democracy, 86–7
Demosthenes, 94
Desire for leadership, 194, 196
Developing leaders, 169–87
 factors in, 182–3
 principles for, 186
 strategy for, 171–2
Developing the individual, 124
Discretionary time, 157
Drucker, Peter, 126, 156, 157
Dunckner, Karl, 88

East Pakistan, 23
Efficiency, 202
Egalitarianism, 8–9, 50
Einstein, Albert, 151
Eisenhower, Dwight D.,
 24, 57, 59,
 86–7, 192
Elected leaders, 44, 85
Emergent leaders, 85
Emerson, R.W., 130–1, 145, 194
Engineering design, 42
Enthusiasm, 54
Equalising recognition, 133–5
Esteem needs, 37
Estimates about consequences, 116
Evaluating, 114–28, 178
 consequences, 114–17
 individuals, 119–26

oneself, 126
team performance, 117–19
Example, setting, 159–66
    for teams and individuals,
        163–5
    in the task area, 159–63
Exercises
    action points, 70–4
    brainstorming, 89–90
    briefing skills, 99
    career profiles, 177
    crisis response, 23, 202
    Elga model, 17–20, 201–2
    frustration of group needs,
        38–9
    hammer problem, 89
    leadership characteristics,
        56–8, 202–3
    leadership motivation, 196
    leadership qualities,
        12–13, 201
    matchsticks problem, 88, 205
    nine dots problem, 88, 205
    observing leaders, 190
    operation self-development,
        197–9
    Regular Commissions Board
        task, 63–4, 204–5
    satisfaction of group needs, 41
Expectations, 74
Experience, 189

Failure, 194–5
Favouritism, 125
Fayol, Henri, 51
Feedback to subordinates, 133
Fiedler, F.E., 32
Financial controls, 109
First impressions, 96
First World War, 100, 136
Fishing trawlers, 161
Flexibility, 21, 24, 52–3
Ford, Henry, 3
Foresight, 91, 208
'Forgotten Army', 134–5
Fragmentation of groups, 118–19
Francis of Assisi, 197
Freedom, individual, 34
Fun, leadership as, 195
Functional approach to leadership,
    51

Functional fixedness, 88
Functioning, level of, 63
Functions of leadership, 43, 50–1

Gibb, C.A., 10, 49
Glubb, Sir John (Glubb Pasha),
    21, 101–2
Goebbels, Joseph, 111
Good, leaders for, 60
Gott, General, 191
'Great man theory of history', 186
Group
    disunity, 39
    frustration, 28
    functions, 29–31, 43
    maintenance, 29, 30–1
    needs, 28–9, 31–3
    personality, 26–8
Group approach to leadership,
    26–48
Group dynamics movement,
    26, 29–30, 34,
    43–4, 45, 50
Gyllenhammar, Per G., 153

Hammarskjold, Dag, 165
Hardy, Thomas, 189
Heap, N., 60
Height, 9
Hersey, P., 32
Herzberg, Frederick, 131–2
Hierarchy of needs, 36
'High-flyers', 173
Hildreth, Jan, 184
Hill, Tony, 116
History and leadership, 170
Hitler, Adolf, 111
Honesty, see Truthfulness
Horrocks, Sir Brian, 122
Human relations, 45, 164
Humanising working conditions,
    153
Humanity, 111
Humility, 54–6, 57, 207
Humour, 55
Hygiene factors, 131–2, 138–40

ICI, 164
Ideas, generating, 90
Imagination, 195–6
Imitation, 164

Impartiality, 125
Inborn qualities, 7–8
Individual needs, 29, 35–8,
    39, 131–2
Individual v. group, 34–5, 38
Industrial democracy, 18
Industrial Society, The, 67–8, 69
Industry, quality of, 202–3
Inferiority complex, 123
Influence, group, 65
Initiative, 55, 209
Innovation, 42, 153
Insight, 185
Instrumental v. expressive
    behaviour, 37–8
Integrity, 11–12, 55
Interaction of needs, 38
Intervention with subordinates,
    106–7
Interviews, 62, 119–24, 172
    pitfalls in, 121
Ismay, Lord, 111
Israelites, 148

Jenkins, W.O., 15
Jesus Christ, 148, 164
Job interest as motivation, 136
Job satisfaction, 131–40, 195
Jones, R.V., 17
Judgement, 52–3, 66, 114–15
    of people, 124–6
Justice, 203

Kipling, Rudyard, 83, 110
Kissinger, Henry, 185
Knowledge, 16–17, 24, 207
Korean War, 50

Lao-Tzu, 106
Lawrence of Arabia, 41
Leadership, short course on, 103
Leadership exercises, 172
Learning, 18, 123, 124
    leadership, 189–90, 196–7
Lee, Robert, E., 111
Le Fanu, Sir Michael, 162
Levels of leadership, 58, 150–1
Lifeboat service, 9
Line managers as leadership
    mentors, 178
Listening, 120

Lord, John, 58
Low profile in leadership, 106
Luck, 191–3

Macgregor, Ian, 99–100
Mcgregor, Douglas, 45, 129–30
Macmillan, Harold, 11, 110
Management
    areas of competence, 176
    consultants, 145–6
    science, 192
Management v. leadership
Managerial Grid, 31–2
Mansell, Anne, 53, 180, 195–6
Marx, Karl, 18
Maslow, A.H., 36–7, 50, 129
Matheson, Ross, 68
Maturity, 32–3
Meetings, controlling, 107–8
Mentors, 124, 178, 191
Military leadership, 21–2, 59, 67,
    93, 96–9, 122
Military tasks, 40–1
Mind, subconscious, 117
Monitoring, 105, 106
Montesquieu, C.-L. de S. de, 87
Montgomery, Viscount, 59, 62, 67,
    68, 96–9, 122, 191
Moore, Michael, 42
Morale, 19, 96–9, 134–5
Moreau, David, 17
Motivating, 35–6, 129–41
Motivators, 131–7, 140
Mountaineering expeditions, 86
Mouton, J.S., 31

Napoleon Bonaparte, 22, 154, 161
Nixon, Richard, 11
Non-verbal behaviour, 30, 108

Objectives, 78–9, 80–1
    in leadership development,
        197–9
Observation, 106
    of leaders, 190–1
Opportunities, career, 181, 192–3
Options, 87–8
Order, 142
Organising, 142–58
    groups, 142–4
    oneself, 154–6

organisations, 145–52
'Outsider', leader as, 172
Over-involvement, 107

Partnership of organisation
  and employees,180
Pasteur, Louis, 193, 194
Patton, George, 59
Paul, St., 110
Performance, improving,
  118–19, 123
Performance information, 73
Perseverence, 55
Personal contact with
  subordinates,100–2, 134–5
Personal example, 159–61,
  162, 163–4
Personal problems, 139–40
Personality, 10
Personnel decisions, 125–6
Persuasiveness, 86–7, 94
Petain, H.-P., 136
Peter Principle, 58
Physiological needs, 36
Pilots, 22
Planning, 83–92
Political constitution of groups, 85
Position of leader, 43–6
Potential, 121, 172, 173, 192
Prepared, being, 192, 193
Principles of leadership, 2, 67, 189
Prior, Peter, 163
Productivity, 70–4
Products, respectability of, 18
Promotion, 176–7
Propertius, 24
Psychological tests, 172–3
Purpose, 78, 79, 80, 81, 151–2
Pygmalion effect, 131

Qualities approach to leadership,
  7–14, 54–6
Quality Circles, 89–90

Reaction, speed of, 22–3
Reasons, giving, 102
Recession, 41
Recognition as motivation, 133–5
Regular Commissions Board, 62–3
Relationships with subordinates,
  45–7, 180, 207

Relaxed atmosphere, 120
Reorganisation, 71–3, 145–6,
  149-50, 152
Research and development, 178–9
Resources
  for leadership development,
    217–18
  for planning, 84
Respect, 46
Responsibility, 44, 209
  as motivation, 136
Restructuring jobs, 154
Results, statement of, 117
Rewarding merit, 137
Ridgway, Mathew B., 10
Roman Army, 46
Roosevelt, Franklin D., 24
Rowntrees, 100
Royal Air Force, 15
Royal Navy, 68
Russell, Lawrence, 119–20

Safety needs, 36
Sandhurst, 64–7
Saunders, Henry, 134
Schein, E.H., 45
Schmidt, W.H., 32–3, 52
Schweitzer, Albert, 188
Scott, J.M., 206–10
Scott, Thomas A., 191
Seaman, Donald, 23, 202
Second World War, 57, 59,
  96–9, 122, 134–5
Security, 138–9
Selection of personnel, 8, 9,
  62–3, 172–3
Self-actualisation needs, 37
Self-confidence, see
  Confidence
Self-control, 109–11
Self-development, 180–1, 188–200
Self-evaluation, 126
Self-fulfilling prophecies, 130–1
Self-motivation, 131
Self-perception, 189, 193
Self-regulation by subordinates,
  106
Self-sacrifice, 164–5
Self-sufficiency, 46
Sharing
  decisions, 51–4, 84

information, 101
Shaw, George Bernard, 3, 131
Shop stewards, 72
Sieff, Lord, 185
Situational approach to leadership, 15–25
Situational factors, 145
Situational leadership theory, 32–3
Size of groups, 71, 142–3, 148–9
Skills, development of, 2
Slim, Viscount, 11, 111, 134–5, 160, 164
Sloan, Alfred P., 88, 126, 142
Small groups, 142–3
Small organisations, 176
Social activities programmes, 27
Social distance, 45–7, 207
Social needs, 36, 46
Social power, 43
Social psychology, 26–7, 31
Social scientists, 8–9
Solidarity, group, 144
Speaking, effective, 94
Spiritual needs, 37
Stability, 63
Standards, group, 118–19
Status, 139
Status barriers, breaking, 163
'Stiff upper lip', 110–11
Stogdill, R.M., 10
Strategic belief in people, 130–1
Structural surveys, 146–9
Structure
    of groups, 142–4
    of organisations, 145, 150–1, 179–80
Style, personal, 53–4
Style of leadership, 31–2
Sub-leaders, 142–3
Summarising, 108
Supervision, 132
Supervisor bonus schemes, 72
Supervisor's workload, 150
Supreme Commander, task of, 59
Symbolic example, 161–3
Sympathy, 139–40

Tact, 55
Tannenbaum, R., 32–3, 52
Task achievement, 28, 38–9, 40
    functions for, 30
T-groups, 26
Thinking
    creative, 42, 87–8, 172–3
    effort of, 117, 125–6
    time for, 155
Thomson of Fleet, Lord, 117
Three-circles model, 33, 38
Time
    availability of, 84
    organising, 154–5, 157
Training, 72, 121
    for leadership, 8, 64–74, 122, 173–5,
    178, 209
Trust, 11, 136
Truthfulness, 11–12, 203
Twelve O'Clock High, 93, 118–19
Two-factor theory, 131–40

Urwick, Lyndall, 51

Values, 12, 58–60
Vision, 173
    sharing, 95–6
Volvo, 153

Wage and salary structure, 72
Waller, General Sir William, 125
Watkins, Gino, 57–8, 206–10
Wellington, Duke of, 91
Whyte, William J., 50
Wisdom, 124
Wordsworth, William, 199
Work, programme for organising, 155–6
Work groups
    and task achievement, 44
    qualities of, 9

Xenophon, 17

Youthfulness, 19

John Adair

Effective Decision Making
A guide to thinking for management success

Few managers devote enough time to the thinking processes they should apply to their jobs. Yet long, energetic hours at work are wasted if business decisions are not logical, clear – and correct.

Effective Decision Making is the definitive guide to the crucial management skill of creative thinking. John Adair draws on examples and case studies from business, recent history, sport and entertainment to show:
• how to approach problems
• imaginative thinking
• sixth sense
• how to argue your case
• how to develop your thinking skills

A complete guide to sharpening your analytical management skills.

John Adair

Effective Innovation
How to stay ahead of the competition

Innovation – the process of taking new ideas through to satisfied customers – is the lifeblood of any organization today. Nothing stultifies a company and the individuals working in it more than a lack of interest in positive change. You cannot stand still: either you go backwards or move forwards.

In *Effective Innovation* John Adair looks at both creativity and innovation: generating new ideas and bringing them to market. His 'seven habits of successful creative thinkers' provides a compelling framework for developing your own productive thinking skills. This readable book also covers leadership of creative teams and discusses how to build an innovative climate in organizations.

A complete guide to a core management competence.

John Adair

Effective Motivation
How to get extraordinary results from everyone

People are the most important asset in any business today. Great results come from great people. Every manager needs to be able to motivate or draw out the best from others, which is not easy in times of corporate change and personal uncertainty.

Effective Motivation is a practical guide to this key leadership skill. Based on a careful evaluation of the research into motivation, John Adair presents a set of strategies for motivating high-performance teams and individuals. Case studies, checklists and exercises help the reader to put the principles behind motivation to productive use.

John Adair

Effective Teambuilding
How to make a winning team

Most tasks in modern business are carried out by teams, so the ability to build and lead them is a vital management attribute.

John Adair has written *Effective Teambuilding* to show how productive working groups can be forged by:
• selecting the right people
• working together
• sustaining group morale
• raising standards of performance

Effective Teambuilding is enriched by a potent blend of examples, anecdotes, case studies and action checklists, all designed to improve team performance.

A supremely practical guide to a vital skill in management.

John Adair

Effective Time Management
How to save time and spend it wisely

Time is a precious resource, both irreplaceable and irreversible. But how can you learn to save time and spend it wisely?

Effective Time Management will help you make the most of every hour. In this unique guide, John Adair, a well-known figure in the management training field, focuses on the time available for daily use using a wide range of examples and case studies, helping to:
• identify long-term goals and middle-term plans
• plan the day and make the best use of your time
• learn to delegate and acquire time effectiveness in the office and at meetings

Effective Time Management will show you how to eliminate time-wasting activities, leaving you with more time for your real priorities.

All Pan Books are available at your local bookshop or newsagent, or can be ordered direct from the publisher. Indicate the number of copies required and fill in the form below.

Send to: Macmillan General Books C.S.
Book Service By Post
PO Box 29, Douglas I-O-M
IM99 1BQ

or phone: 01624 675137, quoting title, author and credit card number.

or fax: 01624 670923, quoting title, author, and credit card number.

or Internet: http://www.bookpost.co.uk

Please enclose a remittance* to the value of the cover price plus 75 pence per book for post and packing. Overseas customers please allow £1.00 per copy for post and packing.

*Payment may be made in sterling by UK personal cheque, Eurocheque, postal order, sterling draft or international money order, made payable to Book Service By Post.

Alternatively by Access/Visa/MasterCard

Card No. ☐☐☐☐☐☐☐☐☐☐☐☐☐☐☐☐

Expiry Date ☐☐☐☐☐☐☐☐☐☐☐☐☐☐☐☐

Signature _____

Applicable only in the UK and BFPO addresses.

While every effort is made to keep prices low, it is sometimes necessary to increase prices at short notice. Pan Books reserve the right to show on covers and charge new retail prices which may differ from those advertised in the text or elsewhere.

NAME AND ADDRESS IN BLOCK CAPITAL LETTERS PLEASE

Name _____

Address _____

_____

_____

_____

8/95

Please allow 28 days for delivery.
Please tick box if you do not wish to receive any additional information. ☐